CROSSING THE STREAM

Also by Sangharakshita

A Survey of Buddhism
The Three Jewels
A Guide to the Buddhist Path
The Essence of Zen
Peace is a Fire
The Thousand-Petalled Lotus *(memoirs)*
Human Enlightenment
The Religion of Art
The Ten Pillars of Buddhism
The Eternal Legacy
Travel Letters
Alternative Traditions
Who is the Buddha?
Ambedkar and Buddhism
The History of My Going for Refuge
The Taste of Freedom
Vision and Transformation
Learning to Walk *(memoirs)*
New Currents in Western Buddhism
The Buddha's Victory
Facing Mount Kanchenjunga *(memoirs)*
The Priceless Jewel
The Drama of Cosmic Enlightenment

The FWBO and 'Protestant Buddhism'
Wisdom Beyond Words
Forty-Three Years Ago
The Meaning of Conversion in Buddhism
Complete Poems 1941–1994
Was the Buddha a Bhikkhu?
In the Realm of the Lotus
Transforming Self and World
Buddhism for Today – and Tomorrow
Ritual and Devotion in Buddhism
The Inconceivable Emancipation
In the Sign of the Golden Wheel *(memoirs)*
Tibetan Buddhism: An Introduction

Booklets

Great Buddhists of the Twentieth Century
Extending the Hand of Fellowship
My Relation to the Order
Mind – Reactive and Creative
Going for Refuge
Buddhism and the West
The Meaning of Orthodoxy in Buddhism

SANGHARAKSHITA

CROSSING THE STREAM

REFLECTIONS ON THE BUDDHIST SPIRITUAL PATH

WINDHORSE PUBLICATIONS

Published by Windhorse Publications
Unit 1-316 The Custard Factory, Gibb Street, Birmingham, B9 4AA

First Windhorse edition 1987
Second edition 1996

Cover design: Dhammarati
Cover picture: Photonica/SOA
Printed by Interprint Ltd
Marsa, Malta

British Library Cataloguing in Publication Data:
A catalogue record for this book is available from the British Library.

ISBN 0 904766 78 0

With the exception of 'Ends and Means', the essays comprising parts 1 and 2 of this book were first published in *Stepping-Stones* between 1949 and 1952, and an edited version of the collection was published in 1972 under the title *Crossing the Stream*. Part 3 was first published by FWBO Publications in 1975 as *The Path of the Inner Life*, and reprinted by Triratna Grantha Mala in 1983.

CONTENTS

About the Author

Sangharakshita was born Dennis Lingwood in South London, in 1925. Largely self-educated, he developed an interest in the cultures and philosophies of the East early on, and realized that he was a Buddhist at the age of sixteen.

The Second World War took him, as a conscript, to India, where he stayed on to become the Buddhist monk Sangharakshita ('protected by the spiritual community'). After studying for some years under leading teachers from the major Buddhist traditions, he went on to teach and write extensively. He also played a key part in the revival of Buddhism in India, particularly through his work among the ex-Untouchables.

After twenty years in India, he returned to England to establish the Friends of the Western Buddhist Order (FWBO) in 1967, and the Western Buddhist Order (called Trailokya Bauddha Mahasangha in India) in 1968. A translator between East and West, between the traditional world and the modern, between principles and practices, Sangharakshita's depth of experience and clear thinking have been appreciated throughout the world.

He has always particularly emphasized the decisive significance of commitment in the spiritual life, the paramount value of spiritual friendship and community, the link between religion and art, and the need for a 'new society' supportive of spiritual aspirations and ideals.

The FWBO is now an international Buddhist movement with centres in sixteen countries world-wide. In recent years Sangharakshita has been handing over most of his responsibilities to his senior disciples in the Order. From his base in London, he is now focusing on personal contact with people, and on his writing.

Foreword

THE ESSAYS GATHERED HERE were written between 1949 and 1952 and made their first appearance in the pages of several important journals: *The Aryan Path, The Middle Way, The Maha Bodhi Journal, The Buddhist,* and *Stepping-Stones.*

For Sangharakshita, this was an extraordinary time, vivid with discovery and inspiration. He began the period as a homeless wanderer in southern and central India; he made his first pilgrimage to the Buddhist holy places; he fulfilled his desire to take ordination as a Buddhist monk; he spent a year studying Abhidhamma and Buddhist logic with Jagdish Kashyap at the Hindu University of Benares. The end of this time saw him installed in the hill-town of Kalimpong, just a few miles from the Tibetan border, where he would remain for fourteen years.

A decade or so later the journey to the East was to become fashionable; an almost commonplace rite of passage for young Westerners thirsty for adventure. In the late forties and early fifties, however, things were very different, and Sangharakshita was very much a lone pioneer. To this remarkable Englishman, who had somehow known himself to be a Buddhist since his teens, India was something more than a reservoir of exotic experience and spiritual (or not-so-spiritual) illuminati, more even than a place of pilgrimage: it was the base from which he would begin his life's work for the future of Buddhism.

His own meditation, study, and insights, as well as some bracing encounters with the Buddhism of Nepal and Tibet, had already convinced him that much of the Buddhism he had encountered in India and Sri Lanka was in a tender state, sadly lacking in spiritual vitality. Ensnared by the conventions of formalistic monasticism, or immersed in the detailed arguments of over-literalistic scholasticism, many people seemed to have forgotten that Buddhism is a living force, a personal communication from an Enlightened being intended to help those who were eager to 'cross the stream', to make the journey from the treacherous quicksands of mundane life to the sure ground of transcendental attainment.

'When he said these words, what was the Buddha really trying to say about the spiritual life?' Meditating in derelict temples and in caves, or pacing the garden of his Kalimpong hermitage, Sangharakshita would bring his mind back again and again to this essential question, pursuing a concentrated search for the practical heart of the Buddha's message. Why did the Buddha choose to speak of *duḥkha* ('suffering' or 'unsatisfactoriness') in his very first sermon? Indeed, why was *duḥkha* the first of his 'four noble truths'? How and why should Buddhists practise tolerance? What does it mean to have no 'self', to overcome the ego, to enter the 'Void'?

Composing issues of his journal, *Stepping-Stones*, he enlisted the vision and committed scholarship of new, and relatively new, names on the Buddhist scene, kindred spirits such as Lama Govinda, Edward Conze, Herbert Guenther, I.B. Horner.... It was time to find a new approach, paradoxically, perhaps, by going back to the heart of things. The future of Buddhism was in the melting pot, and there was so much work to be done. Soon he would compose his acclaimed overview of Buddhist tradition and practice: *A Survey of Buddhism*, and establish the Triyana Vardhana Vihara, the first ever inter-denominational Buddhist centre. In time he would return to the West to found the Friends of the Western Buddhist Order, a new kind of Buddhist movement with the aim of making Buddhism relevant and accessible to people in the modern world. It was in such a mood of heightened idealism, aware that he had crossed the brink of a dazzling spiritual adventure, that he wrote the essays before you now.

Sangharakshita's literary style has changed over the years. But this edition of early writings is willingly offered once again, in the belief that the insights and ideas expressed in these brief passages are as necessary, as vibrant, and as enlightening today as they were when they were first committed to paper.

Nagabodhi

CROSSING THE STREAM

Stepping-Stones

THROUGH THE DEPTHS OF OUR HEARTS flows the dark and tumultuous stream of desire, hatred, and delusion. Noble impulses and sublime aspirations rise bubble-like to the surface of those impetuous waters only to be swept swiftly, helplessly away. No bridge spans that foaming flood, not even the slenderest rope-way hung threadwise from shore to shore, like those which bear the swaying pilgrim across perilous Himalayan gorges. Man sees no way of crossing over from the Hither Shore of his individual, selfish existence to the Further Shore of super-individual, utterly selfless Wisdom and Compassion. Consequently, he either runs up and down the bank seeking in vain for aid or, venturing into the swirling waters, is swept struggling to his doom.

Nor does this threefold stream flow only through the hearts of men. The Enlightened have taught us that the whole so-called objective world, which seems so solid and so real, is only the image of the good and evil in our hearts flung shadow-wise upon the screen of space and time. The steadily rising flood of social, political, and economic ills which is at present threatening to engulf not only all that is noblest in the human heritage, but even humanity itself, is nothing but the gigantic shadow of the raging torrent of desire, hatred, and delusion which is rushing headlong through the hearts of men. We can cross the stream of suffering only by crossing the stream of desire, for in truth the two are one. When we have recognized this fact, we shall no longer run after the superficial panaceas of all sorts of ideological quacks but, withdrawing into the depths of our own hearts, will search diligently for the way to purity, which is also the way to peace and bliss.

Can that Way be found? Never, perhaps, by our own unaided efforts. But One found it many centuries ago, after it had lain for millennia undiscovered and unknown, and having Himself crossed over to the Further Shore, returned to the Hither Shore to proclaim the good news to those who were running blindly up and down the bank. He has pointed out to us the Three Great Stones, wedged immoveably since beginningless time in the bed of that perilous stream, by leaping from which to which a man can cross safely over to the Further Shore of deliverance from old age, disease, and death – the Three Great Stones of Moral Conduct, Meditation, and Transcendental Wisdom. He has also pointed out to us the many other rocks and pebbles wedged between, which, together with the Three Great Stepping-Stones, make up that Great Way, Middle Way, or Āryan Path which spans the stormy waters of Samsaric existence, and across which have gone all the Wise and Compassionate Ones of the past and across which must go all the Wise and Compassionate Ones of the future.

He has discovered the Way, and He has pointed out to us and described the greater and smaller stones which constitute it, but we ourselves must perforce muster courage and resolution to leap from stone to stone across. A keen eye is needed, and steady nerves, on that greatest of all adventures – the spiritual life; for otherwise we shall lose our balance, slip, and fall headlong into the torrent that rages below. Patience is needed too, or else the difficulties we are called upon to face will cause us to give up the attempt in despair; intelligence, or we shall be unable to find our way; faith, or we shall doubt whether the Way in truth exists or whether our Guide had crossed it Himself or not.

Seeing that men are running more blindly than ever up and down the Hither Shore, and with the conviction that only by crossing over the stream of desire, which is at the same time the stream of suffering, can they reach the Further Shore of Enlightenment which is also Compassion and Perfect Bliss, we seek to draw the attention of the modern world to those great Stepping-Stones which our Master discovered. That we can help even a small portion of the world to cross is more than we dare to hope. But if we can help one pilgrim to take even one step across the stream our labours will be richly rewarded and our existence fully justified.

Ends and Means

THE DHARMA WAS NOT INVENTED by the unenlightened mind of a worldly person, but it was discovered and revealed by the fully enlightened consciousness of the Buddha. It is not a mere speculative philosophy, nor a set of theories about man and the universe. On the contrary, it is a path, a method, and a practique which, if faithfully and intelligently followed, will lead the disciple step by step, stage after stage, up the steep and difficult hill of Truth, until at last he stands on the lofty summit even as of old the Buddha stood there, and sees with the undimmed Eye of Knowledge what the Buddha Himself saw – vista upon vista of Wisdom and Compassion without limit in space and without duration in time. If any formal definition of the Dharma is considered necessary, then it is simply 'the means which conduce to Enlightenment'. Contrariwise, anything which does not conduce to Enlightenment is not to be included within the scope of the Dharma or considered as belonging to it in any way. Since it is the presence in our minds of the three 'unwholesome roots' of greed, hatred, and (spiritual) ignorance which causes its original purity to become obscured and prevents us from gaining Enlightenment, the Dharma has often been defined as anything which conduces to the weakening and eventual extinction of these roots, while anything which helps strengthen them and keep them alive is *adharma*. Another supplementary definition states that Dharma is that which is profitable to oneself as well as to others.

'The means which conduce to Enlightenment' are of many kinds, varying as they do in accordance with the widely different temperaments of men and women with different cultural backgrounds and educational qualifications, possessed of different degrees of intellectual acuteness and emotional sensitivity, with stronger or weaker passions, more or less greed, hatred, and ignorance, better or worse health, greater or less familiarity with the difficulties and pains of living. However, human nature is basically the same in spite of the variety of its manifestations; similarly the means which are designed to purify and elevate it are in principle identical amid the rich multiplicity of their forms and applications, and in fact distribute themselves quite naturally into three main divisions. The cultivation of Wisdom is a means to Enlightenment, since Enlightenment is obscured by ignorance. In this division are to be included what are generally referred to as the 'doctrines' of Buddhism, every one of which is an intellectual remedy for a specific intellectual disease. The Doctrine of *anātman* or 'no-self', for instance, is the antidote for the poison of the delusion of an *ātman* or 'self'. Like all the other 'Means to Enlightenment', it is merely an instrument, and apart from the function it is intended to fulfil has in itself no value. The cultivation of Samādhi (in which is included all the degrees of concentration) is a means to Wisdom, and therefore to Enlightenment also, since Wisdom cannot arise in a mind which is perpetually agitated, as the minds of most people generally are. In this division must be placed the numerous exercises which have been designed, whether by the Buddha Himself or by His immediate or remote disciples (or even those discovered by the founders and followers of the various 'religions' of the world, provided they are tested and found really efficacious in calming and concentrating the mind). Buddhism is of unrivalled richness in this particular field. Ethical observances are a means to Samādhi, and therefore to Wisdom and Enlightenment as well, since the performance of actions such as killing, stealing, sexual misconduct, lying, and partaking of intoxicating drinks and drugs will react violently upon the mind of the person who performs them, just as a stone flung into a pool disturbs the tranquillity of its waters, and will strengthen the greed, hatred, and ignorance by which these acts were originally impelled. If they are recapitulated in reverse order these three classes of means will fall into the three progressive stages into which the Path to Nirvāṇa is commonly divided – *sīla* (the practice of morality), *samādhi* (mental concentration), and *prajñā* (liberating wisdom), the second arising in dependence on the first, and the third in dependence upon the second.

Whether or not a particular person enters upon the first of these three stages with the intention of ultimately entering upon the others as well depends to a great extent on previous intellectual understanding of the Doctrine, and whether opportunities for the acquisition of such an understanding exist or not generally depends on whether the environment into which one is born is Buddhist or non-Buddhist. Birth in a Buddhist country is a great advantage, and is rightly regarded as the fruition of meritorious actions performed in previous existences. Even if the Word of the Buddha is extant in a particular country, and facilities for its study are provided there, such a country cannot strictly be termed Buddhist unless its culture, social customs, and political institutions are based upon the Dharma, thus providing an environment which is conducive to the actual practice of the Buddha's teachings. To argue, as some have done, that 'religion' (much misunderstanding would be avoided if the correct term Dharma could be used instead) is a personal concern, and that it therefore has nothing to do with the social and political life of the nation as a whole, is simply to indulge in obscurantism, – where it is not something far more sinister: a deliberate attempt to undermine the influence of Buddhism.

Both objective and subjective factors enter into the conditions upon which the living of the Buddhist life depends, and it would be foolish to ignore either of them. Incidentally, we are hereby furnished with a criterion for social reform: customs which stimulate greed, hatred, and ignorance should be abolished, and those which encourage purity, compassion, and wisdom should be promoted in their place. We have also stumbled upon the strongest of all arguments which can be advanced in favour of giving Buddhist children a Buddhist education, though by this should be understood not a curriculum in which 'Dharma' has been included on the same footing as arithmetic and history, but one based in its entirety on the teachings of the Buddha, and aiming to train Buddhist characters to take their place as members of a Buddhist community. We have moreover discovered the motive which led Buddha Amitābha to establish His Land of Bliss, which was nothing but the compassionate desire to provide a place wherein conditions for the attainment of Enlightenment would be as favourable as possible.

Of course, there are people to whom the idea of dependence of any kind is extremely distasteful, and who maintain with great vehemence that a true Buddhist should be independent of all external aids. It must be observed of them that they have failed to understand the Dharma. One of the most important teachings of the Tathāgata is that nothing arises without at least two causes, a teaching which is no less true of the mental than of the material world. We have already seen that each stage of the path arises not only as a result of direct individual volition but also in dependence upon the whole complex of conditions which constitute the stage preceding it. If we rely for the achievement of Nirvāṇa solely upon our own unaided efforts we shall be like the man who tried to lift himself from the ground by means of his own boot-straps. Whether we choose to recognize the fact or not, it is the presence of certain objective conditions which enable us to lead the holy life. To begin with, if the Dharma was not a law inherent in the very nature of things, if the universe was not so constituted that different causes produce different effects, a certain action an equivalent and equal reaction, and if everything depended instead upon chance, which is say upon nothing, then it would no more be possible for a human being to progress spiritually than it would be for a bird to fly in a vacuum, or for a man to walk without the existence of gravitation. Again, if the sequence of conditions upon which the attainment of Enlightenment depends had not been revealed to the world by the Buddha it is extremely doubtful whether any of us would have ever succeeded in discovering them for ourselves. The independent spirit of those who wish to be entirely free from all external assistance is certainly to be admired, but if they wish to be consistent they cannot be Buddhists, since a Buddhist is one who takes refuge in the Buddha, the Dharma, and the Sangha, and such refuge cannot be taken without surrendering at least a little of one's independence. Moreover, the leading of the holy life depends upon numerous other conditions which the spiritual individualist either overlooks or ignores. It depends, for example, upon the possession of a human body, upon the enjoyment of moderately good health, upon the vicissitudes of climate and weather, on social and political environment, upon whether one meets a 'good friend' or not. All such aids must be relinquished if one intends to achieve Nirvāṇa by the pure unaided exercise of personal volition, in which case the desired achievement should take place instantaneously. There is no doubt at all that if the thrust of our volition were sufficiently powerful Nirvāṇa could indeed be won within the twinkling of an eye. But it is weak, and instead of piercing the dense cloud of ignorance by which the sun of supernal wisdom is obscured, it beats feebly upon it, like a moth fluttering against the window pane. We therefore are compelled to bethink ourselves of how to remove ignorance; but this task also we find beyond our powers, and we are forced to enquire how to bring the oscillations of the mind to a point of perfect balance. In this way we are brought step by step down to dependence upon the simplest supports of the normative life, to dependence upon ethical observances, rites and ceremonies, recitation of prayers, telling of beads, and many other humble and homely religious observances upon which the spiritual individualist looks down with a smile of contempt, but which are nevertheless humanity's first faltering steps upon the Path that leads to Peace. A cripple, however, is certainly not in a position to ridicule a baby's first attempts to crawl; for one day it will walk, while he will be still confined to his bed or chair. Some spiritual individualists do not, indeed, regard external supports to the religious life as being entirely without use, and admit that for some types of people they may be helpful, even necessary; but the admission is generally made in a patronizing and condescending spirit, with the ungracious reservation that supports of this kind are concessions to the deplorable infirmity of people too weak, childish, and spiritually undeveloped to be able to manage without them. Forgetting that it is impossible to tread the Path to Nirvāṇa without some kind of external assistance, some strange perversity of thought constrains them to assert that the spiritual individualist alone is the true Buddhist, although the words of the Buddha Himself afford no warrant whatever for the adoption of such an attitude. Whether one depends for the time being upon meditation, or whether one depends upon the turning of a prayer wheel, the fact of dependence is there, and since both practices are means to an end, which is Enlightenment, neither can be regarded as intrinsically 'better' or 'worse' than any other. It is simply a question of suitability, of the fitness of a particular means for a person of a particular temperament at a certain stage of his or her spiritual development. Similarly, no method is intrinsically 'harder' or 'easier' than any other. Those who believe that they follow the path of self-reliance merely because it is more difficult than the alternative path simply delude themselves. In the spiritual life, as in any other, one naturally takes the line of least resistance. To attain Enlightenment is not such a light undertaking that we can afford to make it more difficult for ourselves than it already is, and if one path was in truth less arduous only pride of Luciferian dimensions could induce us to reject it in favour of another more arduous. Some people, it seems, would rather preserve their independence and remain in the Saṁsāra than renounce it even for one moment and thereby win the bliss and peace of Nirvāṇa. In the spiritual life we have to depend not only upon our own will, our own strength, but also upon a greater or lesser number of external supports most, if not all, of which fall into one or other of the three 'stages' into which the Path has been divided: *śīla*, *samādhi*, and *prajñā*. There is neither absolute dependence nor absolute independence, but a Middle Way which passes between these extremes by escaping into a third dimension wherein the opposition does not exist. For this reason the Buddha has advised us to take refuge in the Dharma, as well as in ourselves, and to regard the Dharma as our light (or island), and not simply to rely, with prideful independence, upon 'our own unaided efforts'.

Just as some misguided people attach little or no importance to the means by which Enlightenment is attained, other equally deluded folk fall headlong into the opposite error, and appear to believe that certain doctrines and disciplines enunciated by the Buddha are ends in themselves, and to be valued for their own sakes, quite regardless of whether or not they do any longer conduce to Enlightenment. This is not to suggest that the Dharma is out of date, or that revolutionary changes in it need to be made. Indeed it should be emphasized that by far the greater part of the methods recommended by the Buddha follow the general laws of human nature, and are therefore of universal validity. Probably the whole of the doctrines which are methods of removing ignorance and producing Wisdom, together with all the practices which are methods of calming the agitations of the mind and achieving Concentration, are conditions upon which the attainment of Enlightenment depends quite regardless of differences of time, place, and temperament. It is in fact in the sphere of *śīla* or ethical observances alone that changes appear to be necessary, and even here the adjustments which are required are by no means drastic, for *śīla* traditionally includes much that would no longer be regarded as pertaining to ethics in the narrower sense of the term, but as being more closely related to what is now included under the terms social customs and etiquette. This is more particularly the case with regard to the numerous and often trivial minor rules which the Buddha laid down during the latter part of His ministry, for the guidance of the Order which He had founded. Each rule was promulgated for a definite reason, the ultimate purpose of them all being to make it easier, not more difficult, for monks to lead the holy life. We are not to imagine the Buddha as sitting down one day and laboriously compiling a long list of dos and don'ts and then imposing them *en bloc* upon the Sangha. Such rules as He did Himself make were strictly contingent in character, and obviously dependent upon factors such as climate, contemporary social customs, local opinion, and popular prejudice. In a totally different set of circumstances it is possible that the Buddha would have made a totally different set of rules. As it was, many of the rules dealing with such matters as the kind of food and dress permitted to members of the Sangha were altered when the torch of the Dharma was carried to lands where climatic conditions vastly different from those of India prevailed. It would indeed have been foolish to expect a monk living in the icy wind-swept uplands of Tibet to wear the thin cotton garment suitable to the semi-tropical climate of the Middle Kingdom, or to maintain health and strength of body on one meal a day. Nor can we admit the plea that it is necessary to appeal directly to the omniscience of a Buddha in order to determine what changes in the existing rules have been rendered desirable by changed circumstances, as it is quite within the competency of ordinary common sense to settle the matter.

Self-evident as the considerations advanced above appear to be, and in spite of the strictness with which they conform to the spirit and letter of the Buddha's teachings, it is nevertheless possible to find within the Buddhist world, notably in a small but of late somewhat vociferous group of Protestant fundamentalists reborn within the orthodox fold, an ignorance of the purely instrumental nature of the Dharma so profound that it is seriously proposed, nay, fiercely and vehemently maintained, that minor monastic rules which are clearly intended to be observed only under conditions similar to those which originally led to their promulgation must be considered as binding upon members of the Sangha in all parts of the world. This is, in effect, to limit the Doctrine and Discipline of the Buddha, which was intended for the welfare of all humanity, to a particular spot on the earth's surface. Even in these favoured lands, however, it would appear that one is considered to be keeping the monastic rules so long as he is not actually discovered breaking them, an attitude which in practice often leads to hypocrisy in one of the most objectionable forms it can assume, when with severely virtuous brow it endeavours to enforce the observance of precepts which in secret it flagrantly violates, and affects to despise those who do in the eyes of the world what they do themselves in the privacy of their own chambers. Many a tale could be told of bhikkhus who exhibit extraordinary indignation if any relaxation of even a single minor Vinaya rule is suggested, but whose cupboards are plentifully stocked with tins of biscuits and jars of jam for their evening meal, – to go no further than that! Even when the Vinaya rules are observed in reality as well as in appearance, however, we not unoften find that they no longer function as means to the realization of Enlightenment. The reason for this apparent lapse of efficacy appears twofold, being due partly to the fact that even in such cases the rules are not observed so much as merely circumvented (as, for example, when a monk abstains from actual physical contact with metal currency, but operates a personal banking account and freely handles cheques and paper money, with the mental attitude that the wealth which these symbols represent is his 'own'), and partly to the fact that in the complete absence of any practically efficacious understanding of the merely instrumental function of all such rules they are regarded as possessing absolute value and 'observed' with such fanatically rigid literalness that the possibility of them serving as a means to the attainment of the remaining stages of the Path is, for the time being at least, precluded. Indeed, it may even be observed that this kind of 'orthodoxy' (as some call it, though in fact it is one of the extremest forms of unorthodoxy), far from being spiritually helpful to those who adopt it, is generally in the highest degree a hindrance to them, and seems to provide an extremely appropriate illustration of what the Buddha had in mind when, using precisely the same word – *sīla* – as for the first stage of the Path, He spoke of *sīlabbata-parāmāsa*, or 'clinging to moral observances and religious vows', a clinging which is, we need hardly add, the third of the ten fetters which a disciple of the Buddha has to break asunder before perfect Freedom can be attained. Moreover, such 'orthodox' monks frequently increase their own mental defilements when, full of arrogant pride, they contrast the 'purity' of their own *sīla* with the 'impurity' of the observances of other monks, and when, their minds replete with hatred and contempt, they attack as 'corrupt' and 'degenerate' all those who seek to observe the spirit as well as the letter of the Buddha's Law, and who do not hesitate to discard minor monastic rules which have become obsolete, and which in some circumstances at least no longer function as supports for the living of the holy life.

Slowly but surely comes the day when the great Banner of the Dharma will have been unfurled in every quarter of the globe, when the deep-voiced drum of the Dharma will have been beaten in every corner of the world, and we have thought it necessary to remind our readers, in the preceding paragraphs, of the true nature of the Message which the Buddha sought to disseminate, not only because of the general importance of the subject, but more particularly because some people appear to be trying to hoist instead the little tinsel flags of local custom and sectarian traditions, while others are with equal enthusiasm beating the battered tin can of exaggerated individualism. Such mistaken endeavours can do, if they can do anything at all, nothing but harm to the great cause which they profess to have espoused, and will be of use only as one more illustration of the famous lines:

He who preached a gospel whereby heaven is won –
Carpenter, or cameleer, or Maya's dreaming son –
Many swords shall pierce him, mingling blood with gall,
But his own disciples shall wound him worst of all.

Broadly speaking, extremists of the first kind are found more often in the East than in the West, while those belonging to the second kind are found more often in the West than in the East. We repeat, not only for their benefit but for the benefit of all Buddhists, whether of East or West – for in the Dharma such differences are of little importance – that the goal of Buddhism is Enlightenment, and that whatever conduces to Enlightenment is to be regarded as the Dharma. The criterion is not theoretical, but practical. Whether we are following the teachings of the Buddha or not cannot be proved or disproved logically; it can be demonstrated only by the purity, compassion, and wisdom of our lives. It should never be forgotten that a means is always a means to a particular end, and the sole test of the validity of any means is whether it does in fact conduce to the attainment of the end for which it was adopted or not. If we bear this principle in mind, we shall avoid, on the one hand, the extreme of dismissing the means to Enlightenment as superfluous, and on the other, the extreme of clinging to them as though they were ends in themselves. Those who at present attach exaggerated importance to the observance of certain minor monastic rules should investigate why those rules were introduced at all, and honestly ask themselves whether, in all cases, they continue to serve their original purpose. Those who are advocates of absolute self-reliance should try to find out whether they are in fact so independent of all external aids as they had imagined, and whether their present self-sufficient attitude is really conducive to Enlightenment. Then it would perhaps be possible for all Buddhists, united in a correct understanding of the Dharma, and following the Middle Way between these and all other extreme views, to co-operate in the work of spreading those principles which are truly the Fundamentals of the Buddha's Message.

The Voice Within

MAN IS TODAY LESS FREE to think and feel simply, naturally, and spontaneously than at any other period in history. The pitiless pressure of education and environment tends to grind down even the feeblest manifestation of independent and original thought or feeling. Our ideas and emotions are manufactured for us by those to whose advantage it is that we should think or feel as they hypocritically tell us it is good for us to think and feel. Lurid hoardings scream at us that this or that particular beverage will give us vitality and strength. Newspaper advertisements assure us with expressions of the fondest solicitude that yet another undreamed-of article is indispensable to our well-being. Political columnists tell us with an air of infallible authority which nation is right and which wrong, while popular orators inform us which ideological group we ought to love and which to hate. The propaganda machines of governments and political parties pour out an incessant stream of ready-made opinions on every possible subject, from the latest international crisis to the most recent scientific discovery. Critics of literature and art, with their 'Book of the Month' and 'Picture of the Year', save us the trouble of having to judge for ourselves which books and paintings deserve our attention and which do not. The synthetic emotion of the latest popular song renders deep and genuine feeling superfluous. Cinemas and radios, newspapers and school text-books, bill-boards and public speeches, together with a thousand other devices for the mass-production and wide dissemination of prefabricated thoughts and emotions, opinions and ideas, are doing man's thinking and feeling for him. He no longer creates, but passively receives the cartoned products of mechanical efficiency. And that which does not create does not live. Man is stunned and deafened by the clamorous pressure of the external. He is no longer master of himself, and therefore no longer master of his environment. His head is full of ideas which he does not truly think, his heart of emotions he does not sincerely feel. A thousand voices from the world without beat upon his ears as relentlessly as the surf upon the sea-beach. The Voice Within is silent.

Not only in the sphere of politics and commerce, literature and art, education and journalism, but in the sacred sphere of religion, also, the same intolerable weight of the external is felt by man. Here, in fact, it has been felt longer than that of almost anything else. The tyranny of cinema and radio, of popular slogan and newspaper advertisement, is a thing of yesterday and today; but the tyranny of religion dates back three or four millennia at least, to the time when divinely-inspired scriptures, infallible prophets, and mediatorial priesthoods made their first attempt to smother the nascent spiritual life of man. As advertisements tell us what to buy, and stump-orators how to vote, so do the Vedas, Bibles, and Korans tell us what to believe, and the prophets and priests who manipulate them, how to invest our money in celestial stocks and shares so as to obtain the largest possible dividends. When the poor investor eventually realizes who really profits from the whole transaction, he may be pardoned if he doubts equally the good faith of his political, commercial, and ecclesiastical advisers! Religious life, instead of being a voyage of spiritual self-discovery, thus becomes an uncritical acceptance of creeds and dogmas which subserve the selfish interests of some particular class or community. Independent thought and unbiased investigation are discouraged and, if possible, suppressed by force, while blind faith (the blinder the better!) is heaped with superlatives and extolled as the one infallible means of obtaining salvation. Divinely-revealed sacred books, infallible prophets, mediatorial priesthoods, and irrefragable dogmas have thundered so loud and long in the ear of humanity that it has been almost deafened by the sound. Once again, the Voice Within is silent or, if not silent, at least unheard.

Buddhism has been described as 'the proudest assertion ever made of human freedom' because it stands up boldly, even defiantly, against the ponderous brute mass of externality that threatens to grind out of existence the moral and spiritual life of man. It not only teaches him that his first duty is to understand things as they really are, but gives him the courage necessary to make the attempt. It exhorts him never to allow himself to be overwhelmed by the flood of thoughts and emotions which come pouring in upon him from all sides, but to weigh and test each one of them in the light of his own knowledge and experience. He should be equally critical of the claims of an advertisement, an election poster, and a religious teaching. That which he finds wrong and harmful he should at once reject, while that which he finds true and good he should accept and endeavour to put into practice. He should in all circumstances think clearly and feel sincerely. Then he will act rightly, too. For Buddhism does not take up such an independent attitude towards the external world simply for the sake of display, but in order to make room for the full development of the latent spiritual-creative powers of man. Pressure from without is wrong and bad only because it crushes the life which is struggling to flower forth from within.

This does not mean that we should allow free play to whatever instincts and impulses happen to spring up within us, but that the purpose of external discipline should be understood before its restraints are accepted. The Buddha said that His disciples should try His words as gold is tried by fire. They were neither to accept them nor reject them without examination. Their confidence in Him should be like that of a patient in his doctor, or of a student in his teacher. The books in which His words have been recorded are not, therefore, regarded by His followers as a revelation in which they must blindly believe, but as a guide to practice with which they may experiment. For this reason Buddhism does not lend itself very easily to the manipulations of priestcraft, and wherever it has remained pure has contributed to the liberation of the creative forces of the human spirit.

When the eyes and ears are blinded and deafened by the very multiplicity of the sights and sounds which come surging in upon them, the mind grows bewildered and independent thought on the situation impossible. The Buddha therefore taught man that if he wants to see things as they really are, if he desires to act nobly and powerfully in the affairs of life, he must first learn to retire within himself and hear, or rather feel, the whisper vibrating through the silence there. He must be his own island of refuge, his own light; he should not look to any external refuge. He should be deaf to all the voices that thunder at him from without so that he can listen to the Voice Within. Then only will he be the master of himself, and master of his environment. Then only will he be able to see and tread the path that will lead him, one day, even to the heart's Enlightenment.

Orthodoxy

THE LAW OF CAUSATION INCLUDES in its majestic sweep every single object of the phenomenal universe. All 'from a molehill to a mountain, an idea to an empire,' live and grow old and die beneath its imperishable dominion, and from its inexorable operation not one is permitted to escape. Written across the face of the heavens in characters of fire, traced in tiny veins on the petals of a flower, and graven deep into the living hearts and minds of men, its enactments govern all things, and the echo of its decrees reverberates in the farthest corners of the universe.

From cause to effect, from mind to matter, from the interior thought to the exterior word and deed, from action to reaction, the sequence is fixed and inescapable: 'All our tendencies of character are the offspring of consciousness, dominated by consciousness, and made up of consciousness. If a man speaks or acts with a sullied consciousness, then suffering follows him, even as the wheel of the wagon follows the hoof of the bullock,' and 'If a man speaks or acts with an unsullied consciousness, then happiness follows him ever, just as his shadow,' roars the Lion of the Śākyas in the fundamental first verses of the *Dhammapada*. A sullied consciousness is one burning with the triple fire of greed, anger, and delusion; an unsullied conscious-ness is one wherein those fires have not only ceased to burn but which is softly aglow with the threefold radiance of purity, compassion, and wisdom.

It is easy to understand, if difficult to practise, the truth that right action cannot issue from wrong feeling, that is to say, from a mind inflamed by lust and rage; but it seems nowadays almost insuperably difficult to comprehend the no less important truth that right action cannot proceed from wrong thinking, from a confused and ignorant state of mind – which in fact underlies and renders possible both desire and hatred – any more than figs can spring from thistles or grapes from thorns. Right emotions which are not backed by right understanding are superficial and unreliable, not constants but variables in the mathematics of character; for while the purity of the mind is sullied by even the slightest vestige of ignorance, of wrong understanding in any of its innumerable forms, the possibility of the recrudescence of desire and hatred cannot ever be precluded.

Those who, seeing the prevalence of wrong action, of flagrant injustice and revolting cruelty, of overt violence and covert oppression, in almost every quarter of the globe today, would seek to put the situation to rights by applying merely the emotional palliatives of love and pity, instead of administering the more astringent medicinal draught of right knowledge, are therefore trimming the twigs of the evil instead of striking at its root. The warm glow of humanitarian sentiment is not intense enough to fuse the world's differences into unity, nor strong enough to beat its angularities straight; for they can be fused only in the fiery furnace of knowledge, and beaten straight only on the anvil of right understanding beneath the hammer blows of insight.

It has become fashionable for the pseudo-intellectual chivalry of our age to tilt a lance at orthodoxy, picturesquely representing it as a sort of dragon from whose clutches the damsel of religion had somehow to be freed. But since the literal meaning of the word orthodoxy is nothing but 'right opinion' or 'correct belief' in doctrinal matters, and since it is this which is basic to right action and right emotion, as we have already shown, it is in fact a return to orthodoxy, to a courageous emphasis on doctrinal fundamentals, to right understanding in all its immaculate purity and uncompromising rigour, of which we stand most desperately in need today. Love is inadequate; goodwill is not enough. The Enlightenment to which, as followers of the Buddha, we aspire, is after all primarily a state of knowledge, and only secondarily and thirdly a type of emotional experience or particular kind of action. It is therefore to Knowledge, to Right Understanding in the fullest sense of the term, to Orthodoxy in the literal sense of the word, that in these dark days we must have recourse if right emotion is to reign in the hearts, and right action in the lives, of men and women the world over.

Unity

THE GREAT SPIRITUAL TEACHERS AND LEADERS of humanity have ever urged us to eliminate selfishness, for this and this alone is the root cause of human bondage and misery from the earliest ages down to the present day. Every living thing feels that it is an infinitesimal speck of selfhood floating perilously on the hostile waters of what is not the self. Each struggles desperately to preserve and build up its own separate individuality in the face of an environment which threatens to destroy it. This attempt, naturally, often brings it into conflict with some at least of all the other millions of struggling selfhoods which are endeavouring to do the same thing, with the result that from the lowest to the highest forms of sentient existence, and particularly in the social, political, and religious life of man, we find that mutual strife, competition, and conflict are the order of the day. It is a strange irony that even Buddhism, the central doctrine of which is that the 'I'-concept is the root cause of the suffering of sentient beings, should be divided by sects professing the same beliefs and individuals working for the attainment of the same ends. So easy is the recognition of truth, so hard its realization!

The Buddha taught clearly and without the possibility of any misunderstanding save that which is conscious and deliberate, that without breaking down the 'narrow domestic walls' which divide the subject from the object, the self from the not-self, one class or one nation from another, and allowing them thoroughly to interpenetrate each other, there can be neither peace in the hearts of men nor happiness on earth. War threatens to embrace the earth once more in its fiery arms simply because nations imagine themselves to be separate entities isolated from the rest of the world and strive to achieve their individual ends regardless of the good and welfare of the whole of which all are, equally, parts. The dove of peace cannot build her nest in the branches of a tree round whose trunk is coiled the triple-headed serpent of selfishness. She builds only on the Jewel Tree of Perfect Interpenetration, where each shining leaf mirrors every other, and where each jewel-fruit reflects the image of the whole tree.

The inevitable result of the 'I'-concept is the world as we see it before our eyes today, a place of fear and suspicion, of covert or overt strife in every sphere of human activity and enterprise, of insurmountable walls and barriers set up between one man, one class, one nation, one religion and another, of distinctions and differences in every walk of life, of mutual exclusions and impenetrabilities – in short this world of suffering which we call Saṁsāra. But the fruit of that utter emptiness of all 'I'-concept which we designate the Voidness is that glorious ideal world of mutual interpenetration described in such lavish detail and with such a wonderful glow of colour in the great Mahāyāna Scriptures. There all the illusory separative walls are broken down and everything melts and joyously flows as it were into every other thing like the mutual interpenetration of innumerable beams of coloured light, or like the mutual reflection of all the different jewels on the magic jewel-net of Indra, thus making what we call the *dharmadhātu*, the Realm of Truth, or the Western Land of Bliss, the Pure Land of Amitābha.

It should not be thought that the world of suffering is in one place and the Realm of Truth in another, for both are in the mind. The consciousness which is defiled by the 'I'-concept lives in a world of desire and therefore, inevitably, in a world of suffering also. Only the consciousness which is free from all taint of selfhood lives in the world of emptiness and compassion and therefore in the world of perfect bliss as well. The kind of world in which we live is simply the exteriorization of the kind of thoughts which we cherish. Hence it has been said that Buddhas and Māras are nothing but the objectification of our own holy and unholy thoughts respectively. The transmutation of the dull dross of greed, hatred, and delusion into the shining gold of purity, compassion, and transcendental wisdom will transform this world of suffering into the Land of Bliss of Amitābha. There is no other way.

The most natural centre for the practice of selflessness is among the disciples of Him who taught utter selflessness. Its most natural outward manifestation should be in the temporal organization of those who profess to follow in their inner spiritual life this above all other teachings of the Master. But owing to a variety of factors such is far from being the case. The followers of the Buddha are split into numerous sects which are, if not actually hostile, at least indifferent to each other. There is lacking that joyous fellowship which should characterize a great brotherhood of believers. Sect remains coldly aloof from sect and community icily indifferent to community. But there are signs, for those who can see and understand what they see, that such will not long be the case. The whole Buddhist world is slowly but surely awakening into new life. Buddhist countries and communities everywhere are becoming more and more alive to the imperative necessity of a common life in the Dharma. *Maitrī*, the very life-blood of Buddhism, is beginning to circulate through every part of the Buddhist world-body. The time is surely not far distant when a single Buddhist Church Universal will mirror to a war-torn world at least a faint image of that ideal realm of peace and bliss which is the infallible result of a common life of utter selflessness.

Rights and Duties

It has been truly said that he who can bear to live alone is either a beast or a god. Most men, however, being neither wholly beast nor wholly god, but a combination of varying proportions of both natures, are unable to live unto themselves in solitude either brutish or divine, and consequently enter into various kinds of relations with other individual men and groups of men. Thus the various domestic, social, civic, political, cultural, and religious relationships in all their bewildering complexity and intricacy of organization arise.

These relationships are not static, like the relations which subsist between the three angles of a triangle, but are dynamic, involving processes of challenge and response, of unceasing mutual adjustment and readjustment. For we are here dealing not with dead unchanging concepts, but with living and therefore continually changing and developing human personalities. The relation which subsists between the lines and angles of any geometrical figure is unalterably fixed for all time; but human relationships are being constantly expanded and deepened, developed and enriched, because the human psyche is itself in a process of constant flux and therefore in constant need of adaptation to its environment. The relation between human beings is, therefore, to be compared not with that of trees standing motionless side by side in the forest, but rather with the unceasing rhythmical movement of a party of dancers, the mutual relations between whom are fluid and in a process of constant change, the advance of one implying the retreat of the other, the clockwise movement of those forming the outer ring the anti-clockwise movement of those forming the inner ring, and so on. For human relationships are not only reciprocal but complementary. The concept of father cannot exist without the complementary concept of child, and the idea of a ruler is meaningless without the corresponding idea of subjects for him to rule over. The two ends, so to speak, of a human relationship are in fact as inseparable as the two ends of a stick. Just as we may run our hand either from the top to the bottom, or from the bottom to the top, of the stick, so in human relationships we may proceed either from ourselves to others or from others to ourselves, considering either what is owed by us to them or by them to us. The first comprise what we call duties, the second what we call rights. But the relationship nevertheless remains in itself an indivisible whole.

The idea of rights without duties or duties without rights is, therefore, an absurdity, a palpable contradiction in terms; for the 'two' are in reality one, being nothing but the same object looked at from different points of view, approached from opposite ends. But just as, in the case of a walking-stick, although its two ends are inseparable, so that one is unthinkable without the other, it is nevertheless the handle of the stick that must be grasped, and not the tip, so in human relationships it is duties that must be performed, rather than rights that must be demanded, even though the two are in fact inseparable so that the one necessarily follows from the other.

Duties consist in what is due from us to others, and are based upon giving, whereas rights consist in what is due from others to us, and are based (from the subjective point of view) upon grasping and getting. The performance of one's duty does not mean merely the grudging recognition and half-hearted rendering of what is legally or even morally due to one's family and friends, social or national group, political party, or religious organization, but in the unobstructed outward flow of one's love and compassion over the whole world. Duty is not, as the poet apostrophizes her, the 'Stern daughter of the Voice of God', but the sweet child of the realization of emptiness – Śūnyatā – within the depths of our own heart. The conscientious performance of one's duties to mother and father, child and wife, friends and acquaintances, masters and disciples, and to the complementary halves of all the other human relationships in which we are inevitably involved, results in the gradual loosening of the bonds of selfishness and egotism. The word for duty and the word for religion (which consists at bottom in the eradication of the ego-sense) are, in the language of India, one word: Dharma. But the clamorous insistence upon our rights, upon what is legally, morally, or even spiritually due from others to us, only strengthens greed, strengthens desire, strengthens selfishness, strengthens egotism.

The performance of one's duties results in the establishment of love and peace, the attempted extortion of one's rights in the outbreak of hatred and violence. Duties unite, rights divide. Duties are co-operative, rights competitive. The former depend upon our own selves, and are therefore swift and easy of accomplishment; the latter depend on others, and are therefore tardy and difficult, if not impossible, of achievement. Rights are wrested forcibly from other human beings outside, but duties are softly and sweetly laid upon us by the voice of the Divine – of our own potential Buddhahood – reverberating within.

Buddhism, being based upon the realization of emptiness, upon egolessness, upon unselfishness, teaches the doctrine of the mutual interpenetration of all things, inculcates the practice of love and compassion, exhorts men and women to perform their duties in every walk of life, and therefore tends naturally towards the ultimate establishment of peace, both in the hearts and minds of men and in the world of events outside us.

Western political systems, on the contrary, however different or even antagonistic they may outwardly seem, are all based upon the concept, ultimately of dogmatic Christian origin, of the existence of separate, mutually exclusive ego-entities which are socially, politically, and even spiritually valuable and significant in themselves. All such systems therefore justify hatred and excuse violence, all insist on the intrinsic reasonableness of clamorous agitation for rights, and all therefore, without exception – despite emphatic protestations to the contrary – result in the eventual outbreak of war, both in the individual psyche and in the life of societies and nations. Emptiness, egolessness, the performance of duties, and internal and external peace and harmony, are members of the same Nirvāṇic series, just as egotism, individualism, the claiming of rights, and external violence and warfare are the indissoluble links of the same Saṁsāric chain.

The world today truly needs peace, but does not sincerely desire it. For peace is sought not in the dynamic equilibrium of selfless mutual performance of duties, but in the mechanical manipulation of merely superficial and therefore unstable adjustments between a host of conflicting egotistic claims. There can be peace in the world between men and between nations only when the hidden roots of disharmony – the concept of a separate soul, self, or ego – are ruthlessly dug up and cast into the blazing fire of selflessness. There can be peace in the world only when doing one's duty is stressed more emphatically than getting one's rights, when it is considered more intrinsically valuable to confer a benefit upon one's fellow men than to receive one from them. It is no more possible to get peace by means of the egotistic assertion of rights than it is possible to gather grapes of thistles or figs of thorns. But peace springs naturally and spontaneously from duties quietly and unobtrusively done, just as from the rose tree comes the rose, or as the lotus rises from the lotus lake.

'But', some will protest, 'if we simply perform our duties, without demanding our rights in return, we shall be taken advantage of and exploited by unscrupulous politicians and crooked capitalists; we shall be abused and trampled upon by people on every side.' This objection would be valid only if the performance of duty were envisaged as something which applied not to all sections of society, but to some only. But since the two ends of a human relationship are as inseparable as the two ends of a stick, and since our rights become duties when looked at from the other end, and since no one will consider himself to be without rights, the performance of duties is an obligation which rests equally upon the shoulders of all men and from which none can escape. The remedy for any injustice or inequality in human relationships, whether domestic, social, civic, political, cultural, racial, or religious, is not an insistence upon the rights of one party, but on the duties of the other. The reminder of their duties appeals to all that is best and noblest in men and nations, to their innate selflessness and love; whereas the reminder of their rights appeals to all that is basest and worst in man, to his innate selfishness and greed, hatred, and violence. The appeal to the performance of duties is constructive and positive, and results in co-operation, harmony, and peace. The appeal to the claiming of rights is destructive and negative, and issues eventually in competition, discord, and open war. The former is based upon the Wisdom and Compassion of all the Buddhas, the latter upon the sophistry and mutual antagonism of the founders of the various schools of Western political thought. One is profound, the other superficial; one transcendental, the other mundane.

If men all did their duty to one another it would not be necessary even to speak of rights. For it is a paradoxical but nevertheless profoundly true fact that all men will get their rights only when all men do their duties, although the converse of this proposition does not necessarily follow. If all fathers perform their duties towards their children it will hardly be necessary for the children to clamour for their rights. Buddhism, which has justly been hymned as 'The wisdom that hath made our Asia mild', exhorts us to perform our duties rather than to struggle for our rights. Is it too much to hope that humanity will pause upon the threshold of a third world war and, before it is too late, hearken to the great teaching of emptiness, selflessness, and compassion, and at last learn to take hold of 'the right end of the stick'?

Everything That Lives is Holy

It is one of the great paradoxes of human life that religion, which was intended primarily as the means of eradicating egotism, should have become one of the most powerful agents for augmenting it. The reason for this apparent anomaly is not far to seek. So deep-rooted in human consciousness is the ego-sense, so tenacious of existence that, like a weed that flourishes equally well in a stony or a fertile soil, it does not hesitate to batten upon any kind of thought or action – even upon those which are conventionally regarded as good, holy, pious, religious, and spiritual. The ego-sense which has succeeded in entrenching itself behind the ramparts of mere formal piety, or outward religiosity, is often more impregnable to the assaults of Light than is the heart of the habitual so-called sinner who has not a shred of 'righteousness' with which to cover the natural nakedness of his egoity. We are all familiar with the somewhat irritating, but really rather pitiable, spectacle of a man who not only prides himself on his abstention from some petty indulgence such as cigarettes or coffee, but actually flaunts the virtue of his abstention in the faces of his friends. Although such people have understood that a certain habit or action is useful to the development of the spiritual life, they have not understood that it ceases to be useful, and becomes instead positively harmful, as soon as one begins to think of it as a virtue, and to regard that virtue as a possession which differentiates him from others who do not possess it. For this reason the conventionally 'good' man is often a harsh and unsympathetic character, critical in the extreme of the faults of others, and highly conscious of the magnitude of his own virtues; while the conventionally 'bad' man or woman may, on the other hand, be sympathetic and unselfish to a degree which almost compensates for his or her deviations from the accepted standard of behaviour. The ego-sense, like some evil contraband, succeeds in smuggling itself across the frontiers which divide, or are supposed to divide, the realm of 'good' from the realm of 'bad' thoughts, words, and deeds. Irreligion dons the garment of religion, the devil the dazzling raiment of an angel of light, and thus the ego's merry masquerade continues.

As within the narrower sphere of the individual, so within the wider sphere of the group. It is possible for the ego to appropriate 'good' actions and 'religious' practices, for a man to flatter himself with the comfortable conviction that he has 'gained' something of a spiritual nature, simply because society has got into the habit of regarding certain actions as good, certain practices as religious, and certain attainments as spiritual, *in themselves*, without reference to the state of consciousness by which they are inspired. Whereas the truth of the matter is that a particular action, practice, or attainment is truly moral, religious, or spiritual only to the extent that it succeeds in eradicating the ego-sense. We should beware of those good deeds which beget too acute an awareness of our own goodness. Or rather, we should beware of the ego-sense which so insidiously introduces itself even into the very heart of our spiritual life and its activities. This is not to say that any action whatsoever may or may not be accompanied by ego-sense and that, therefore, any action whatsoever is capable of being either spiritual or unspiritual in the true sense of the term. Such a statement would amount to a defence of antinomianism, of the ludicrous theory that since a liberated being has transcended the moral law he may transgress it with impunity. Although it is true that no action is in itself good or bad, but only in so far as it is inspired by a selfish or a selfless consciousness, there is nevertheless a class of actions (to which belong murder, theft, adultery, etc.) which are invariably the product of the ego-sense and which cannot possibly be performed without it. Because the presence or absence of ego-consciousness is the true criterion of the spiritual value of an action, we should not fall into the error of supposing that any action, however immoral according to the consensus of religious opinion throughout the ages, can be performed without it and thereby assume spiritual status.

Society has, unfortunately, acquired the habit of regarding certain actions, such as attending a temple, church, or mosque, or visiting a place of pilgrimage, as religious in themselves, without reference to the background of consciousness which stands behind them. Similarly, certain occupations or avocations, such as those of the monk or priest, are regarded as possessing, in some almost magical fashion, a peculiar virtue or sanctity. Particular places, buildings, costumes, books, languages, countries, colours, and so on are, in exactly the same way, set apart as sacred from the mass of profane objects of the same class by which they are surrounded, and from which they are so sharply distinguished. The result of this dichotomization of things into sacred and profane is an unhealthy division of the collective or social consciousness analogous to the split produced in the individual consciousness by its arbitrary classification of actions as 'good' and 'bad'. This is not to deny the power which is certainly possessed by certain external places and objects of inducing corresponding states of consciousness internally. This is because we have, either by deliberate individual choice or by passive acceptance of the cultural or religious tradition into which we are born, come to regard some material thing as the symbol of a spiritual value. But the sacredness or profaneness of that thing nevertheless continues to depend upon the state of mind which it is capable of inspiring. If a 'holy' object no longer inspires holy thoughts then it ceases to be a symbol and becomes a superstition. For the very essence of superstition consists in regarding things – whether particular persons, places, or practices – as holy in themselves, without reference to the state of mind which accompanies them. That thought, word, or deed alone is holy concerning which the idea that 'I am the doer' does not arise.

The most unfortunate practical consequence of regarding things as in themselves sacred or profane is that the vast mass of people consider themselves to be totally excluded from participation in the practice of religion. Religion, they think, belongs to the temple or church, not to the home, to the priest, not to the layman. It can be found within the covers of some musty book, but not among the flowers that bloom so freshly in the fields, or in consort with the 'lutes that whisper softness in chambers'. Priests and ecclesiastical bodies of every religious denomination have not only deliberately encouraged, but even sedulously inculcated, this wrong attitude of mind, in order to strengthen their positions and swell their revenues. But the truth of the matter is that you cannot see anything as holy until you see everything as holy. Distinctions are useful, even necessary, at the beginning of one's spiritual career; but they should not be clung to. A flower is sacred, a tree holy, if you look at it with an illumined mind, just as a religious observance is profane if you do it with a greedy, malicious, or deluded consciousness. It is better to sweep a floor egolessly than to meditate with the prideful sense that 'I am meditating.'

Swinging thus the emphasis from the external to the internal, from the act to the thought, from the symbol to the thing symbolized, we can see that religion is not confined to particular places, but that it saturates and sanctifies the whole of nature;

that it is, properly understood, not for the few only, but inevitably and inescapably for all; and that there is, to the Eye of Enlightenment, no division between sacred and profane but that, in the words of a great poet-seer, 'Everything that lives is holy.'

LIVING IN THE PRESENT

THE PROVERBIAL EXHORTATION not to put off till tomorrow what one can do today reminds us of the readiness with which imagination loses itself not only in the future but in the past as well. 'We look before and after, and pine for what is not,' sings the poet; and it is significant that the forward look and backward glance should be associated with pining for – that is to say, desiring – that which is not or – what amounts to the same thing – that which is unreal. Wherever desire for the ephemeral pleasures and transitory possessions of the world exists, there will exist also regret for them when they are past, and hope for their fulfilment and fear of their disappointment while they are yet to come. Desire diffuses the attention of man over the beginninglessness of the past and the endlessness of the future, thus weakening his power of concentration and impairing his efficiency in dealing with the problems of the present as they arise.

When, therefore, such desire becomes gradually less, regret, hope, and fear diminish in a corresponding degree, and the spiritual aspirant tends less and less to live either in recollections of the past or anticipations of the future, and more and more in the present life, the passing hour, the immediately apprehended point-instant of his experience. He fulfils the exhortation of the Buddha: 'Renounce what lies in the future, give up that which is past, and surrendering the present, cross to the other shore. With a mind thus entirely freed, you will no more fall into birth and death.' Hence the childlikeness, the seeming irresponsibility, and apparent frivolity, even, of the truly spiritual man, who is said in the Scriptures to be incapable of laying up today even the food which he will need for the morrow. Since he finds in the present a source of inexhaustible satisfaction and perennial joy he has no need of either a regretful backward glance at the past or an anxious or hopeful one forward to the future.

It should not be thought, however, that the spiritual man lives in the present in the same sense as the worldling does. The former lives in the present because he is free from desires, and therefore free also from hope and fear; whereas the worldling lives in the present because his desires are so importunate that he neglects in satisfying them even considerations of worldly prudence, plunging instead headlong into the torrent of enjoyment without a thought of whither it will sweep him in the end. The saint's surrender to the demands of the present, and the worldling's abandonment of himself to the seductions of the passing hour, resemble each other as much and as little as darkness which is excess of light resembles darkness which is mere privation of light. For whereas the spiritual man not only renounces what lies in the future and gives up that which is past, but also surrenders the present, the carnal man on the contrary clings to the present as the bee clings to a flower, seeking to extract from it not only the last drop of its own sweetness but the honeydews of past and future as well. Consequently, whereas the spiritual man crosses in the end to the Other Shore, the carnal man remains bound in the shallows and miseries of this shore.

To the saint the experiences of the passing hour are not valuable or significant for their own sake, but only in so far as they are capable of functioning as conduits for the inflowing power and energy of That wherein past, present, and future are not, so that the incessantly celebrated rite of the temporal present is transformed into a series of infinitely varied sacraments of the

Eternal Now, through every one of which is revealed an aspect of that inexhaustible richness which will be experienced in its plenitude only with the attainment of Supreme Enlightenment. Whether the experiences of the present moment be tinged with joy or pain, whether born laughing from the sweetness or wailing from the bitterness of human relationships, or whether arising out of the depths of contemplation aesthetic or religious, the saint seeks to taste through them all that Nectar for which he thirsts indeed, and to experience that Simultaneity to which and in which, while seemingly immersed in the flow of the present, he lives above and beyond the past, the present, and the future.

THE PROBLEM OF DESIRE

IT IS AGREED BY ALL SECTS AND SCHOOLS of Buddhism that the elimination of desire is the principal desideratum of the spiritual life. For it is by thirst, craving, or desire for the fascinating but transitory mirages of sense- and mind-objects that we are led unawares into the midst of the burning desert of pain. Nirvāṇa, the goal of the aeon-long path of spiritual aspiration, is, negatively speaking, nothing but the complete and final extinction of the fierce red flame of desire in the cool translucent waters of desirelessness. All the tropically rich profusion of religious practices and methods of spiritual training which have sprung up, in the course of centuries, from the fertile soil of the Buddha Dharma have, as their final fruit, their sole aim, and ultimate objective, nothing but this – the utter annihilation of desire.

'But', protest some, 'if we eliminate desire altogether, even the desire for things which are pure and holy, such as the desire to dedicate our lives to the service of humanity, or the longing to realize Nirvāṇa, then we shall be deprived of all incentive to lead a good life rather than a bad one, and the practice of religion will be rendered impossible. For religion to demand the complete annihilation of desire is like a man asking that the branch of the tree on which he is sitting should be cut off. Religion is self-destructive. Desire cannot be annihilated without the *desire* for the annihilation of desire. Therefore religion is utterly impracticable. Better to relegate it to the rubbish heap.' Thus argue some.

The difficulty arises, as such difficulties usually do arise, from the lack of a precise and accurate definition of the meaning of the term around which the whole discussion revolves. None of the protesters and objectors who raise such a hubbub about 'desire' really know what they are talking about. We are not being rude. We are simply stating a plain fact in plain words. They think that because a word is freely used in popular parlance the meaning of it is perfectly clear to all concerned. But the truth of the matter is that they utter the word with their tongues without having in their minds anything more than the haziest idea to correspond with it. What we are really concerned with is not so much the problem of desire as the problem of the definition of desire.

It must be admitted, to begin with, that the word 'desire' signifies a world of experience which contains two distinct, and, indeed, quite contrary, hemispheres of meaning. For the first may be reserved the exclusive right to the use of the term 'desire', and for the use of the second we may appropriate the term 'aspiration'. The difference between the two consists at bottom in their relation to the ego-sense. Both desire and aspiration are emotions, they belong to the feeling-aspect of man's complex psychological constitution, they are essentially dynamic and more of the nature of impulsions or urges than of the nature of understanding. But the similarity between them does not go beyond this point. For whereas desire is based upon the ego-sense and all its activity is a circular and contractive movement of return thereto, aspiration is based upon the idea of non-ego and all its activity is a spiral and expansive movement of ascension towards that absolute emptiness of self which is at the same time the fullness of Compassion. Desire is the motive power which makes the Wheel of Birth and Death revolve; but aspiration is the propulsive force which bears the aspirant upstream to Nirvāṇa. The former is the direct antithesis of the latter. If the spiritual life consists negatively in the elimination of desire, it consists positively – and the positive is always more important than the negative, which it in fact includes – simply in the unflagging cultivation of aspiration. The so-called problem of desire arises only when this one term is used to describe two diametrically opposite modes of psychic progression. But if the term 'desire' is used exclusively for one mode of progression, and the term 'aspiration' for the other, the whole difficulty melts away like mist at sunrise. No wonder, then, that according to Confucius the 'rectification of terms' was the first task to be undertaken by the social and religious reformer!

We have already seen that one of the evil effects of not making a clear distinction between desire and aspiration – throwing instead all emotional impulses together into one untidy heap – is to make many people dismiss religion as quite impracticable. Another evil effect is that it tends to make religion, even for those who do believe in it and who try to practise it, such a drearily negative affair that they find in it neither life nor joy – to say nothing of Enlightenment. Under the mistaken influence of a neat little syllogism that since all desire is evil and since all emotion is desire, therefore emotion is evil and must be eliminated, they unintentionally frustrate the whole course of their spiritual life by stultifying the one impulse which is able to endow it with sufficient velocity to reach its goal. The repressive or merely ascetic type of religion (condemned by the Buddha as one of the extremes which the follower of the Middle Way must avoid) has always been afraid of emotion instead of boldly facing it and endeavouring to utilize it to the advantage of the spiritual life. It has failed to realize that only on the wings of purified and spiritualized emotions of love and compassion can the spiritual aspirant soar high into the empyrean realms of Emptiness, just as it is only by means of keen-eyed knowledge and wisdom that he is able to find his way thereto. Spiritual life is no more possible without emotion than it is possible without understanding. The Bodhisattva, or ideal spiritual aspirant, is therefore represented as being simultaneously the embodiment of infinite wisdom and of boundless compassion. It may, in fact, even be said that the criterion of our having truly *understood* the illusoriness of the ego-conception is whether or not we are able to *feel* for the sufferings of others that 'painless sympathy with pain' which is, according to Buddhist teaching, the natural and spontaneous outward expression of all true spiritual attainment. Freedom from desire consists not in marble-hearted insensitivity to human suffering but in that warm and ready response to it which only desirelessness – that is to say, unselfishness – is able to make. Only those who are truly desireless know how to love, and in universal love lies the secret of liberation.

But here, as elsewhere in the spiritual life, we must beware lest the instincts of our lower nature succeed in masquerading as the intuitions of our higher nature. We may only too easily delude ourselves that we are cultivating love and compassion when we are in fact increasing our desires and attachments. The only way in which we can sort out the threads of love and desire entangled in our hearts is closely to scrutinize each emotion as it arises and observe whether it strengthens or weakens the ego-sense, whether it results in generous giving or selfish accumulation, and whether it brings at the end the peace and calm of content or the pangs of disappointment and frustration. 'By their fruits ye shall know them,' said one who was in many ways the faithful disciple of the Buddha. The bitter fruit of desire is pain – even of the desire for Nirvāṇa, if by this we mean the selfish hankering to possess it exclusively for the sake of one's own personal gratification; but the sweet fruit of love is liberation – not for oneself alone but for all sentient beings. It is this

great mystery which lies at the heart of the Bodhisattva's 'renunciation' of Nirvāṇa. He renounces it not as an object of
aspiration, but as an object of desire. Leading a spiritual life does
not consist in *gaining* Enlightenment *for* the self, but in the death
of the self which is Enlightenment – that 'Enlightenment for the
sake of all sentient beings' which is the goal of the Bodhisattva's
career.

He who has solved the problem of desire has solved the
problem of love – if love is a problem, except to those who have
it not – and those who have solved the problem of love have
solved, also, the problem of life itself. Such live 'in the world,
but not of it', like the white lotus unsullied by the mud wherefrom it grows 'for the good of the many, the happiness of the
many', knowing and feeling every moment of their lives that
aspiration is better than desire, love and compassion more
blessed than attachment, and that it is in truth greater bliss to
give than to receive.

THE GOOD FRIEND

TO THE EMPEROR OF CHINA'S ENQUIRY as to what constituted the essence of Buddhism the Indian sage Bodhidharma replied that it consisted in abstention from all evil, doing of good, and the purification of one's heart. This reply failed to satisfy His Imperial Majesty, who apparently had expected to hear something extremely abstruse and esoteric, and he therefore observed, not without a trace of sarcasm, that the teaching was so simple that even a child of three could understand it. 'So simple that a child of three can understand it, but so difficult that even an old man of eighty cannot practise it,' retorted the sage. The moral of the story is clear: intellectual understanding and practical realization of a religious doctrine are rarely commensurate. Nor is the reason far to seek. Reluctant as he may be to admit the fact, man is after all a creature of desires rather than the child of reason; and it is by his emotional attitude to any particular subject or situation, rather than by his intellectual understanding of the issues involved therein, that the course of his conduct is ultimately determined. Reason may point man to the stars, but so long as his desires continue to drag him earthward among the glow-worms of the grass he is powerless to reach up and pluck even the lowest and least of them from the azure depths of its native sky. The central problem of the spiritual life is, therefore, as we have said elsewhere, not static but dynamic, not so much a matter of the intellectual understanding of this or that doctrine as of the concentration of the total psychic energy of the individual – now dissipated in so many directions – along the line of its eventual realization. Since this energy is nothing but the energy of desire in the widest possible sense of the term, and since emotion is only the 'long-circuiting' of desire, it is with the concentration and sublimation of desire and the reorientation of emotion that the spiritual life is above all else concerned.

Such is the case with the doctrine of no-self. Difficult as it is to understand that things are void of soul, self, or ego, to put the doctrine into practice is more difficult still, to realize it most difficult of all. For no matter how clearly the intellect may be able to conceive this or any other doctrine, while the individual remains uninvolved with it emotionally all his intellectual understanding is as useless as a locomotive without fuel. The difficulty which confronts the spiritual aspirant is not so much how to understand the doctrine of no-self as where in his experience to discover the rudimentary form at least of its emotional equivalent.

Desire is of two kinds, that of attraction, the desire to unite, and that of repulsion, the desire to separate. When the former is accompanied by an intellectual cognition of an object which is inferior, equal, or superior to itself, it becomes differentiated into the emotions of compassion, love, and adoration respectively, each of which may in turn be divided into two kinds, one selfish inasmuch as it seeks to merge the being of the object in its own, the other selfless inasmuch as it seeks to merge its own being in that of the object. While sex-love is the most typical emotional form assumed by selfish desire to unite (which explains, incidentally, the ease with which such love passes over into hatred), what we may designate as friendship-love, or simply friendship, is the most typical emotional form of selfless desire to unite. It is, therefore, in friendship (the Buddhist virtue of *maitrī*) and the sentiments kindred to it that, among all the relationships of human life, we may find in its rudimentary form at least the emotional equivalent of the intellectual understanding of the doctrine of no-self.

The emotion of friendship manifests in daily life as a readiness to sacrifice one's own pleasure and profit for the pleasure and profit of another, as a willingness to go where and do what is agreeable to him rather than to oneself; while at its most exalted height it manifests as that supreme act of self-abnegation whereof it is written 'Greater love hath no man than this, that he lay down his life for his friend' – a text whereto more than one Jātaka might serve as commentary. But behind every mani-festation of friendship, of *maitrī*, from the lowest to the highest, lies, as the heart-beat behind the rhythm of the pulses, the central psychological fact of the more or less radical denial of the selfish individual will; and it is due to the presence of this partial negation of selfhood, of the joyous merging of one's own being in the being of another, that friendship and its kindred emotions are so richly endowed with potentialities for spiritual development.

If, however, those potentialities are to be actualized, it is necessary to cultivate, during the formative period of one's spiritual career at least, the friendship of the good rather than of the wicked. For with those whom we love we shall naturally tend to associate as often and as intimately as possible, delight-ing to go where they go and do what they do, which means that if our friends are slaves of vice their company will ultimately make us vicious, while if they are servants of virtue we may by their example and influence one day become virtuous. It is for this reason that the Buddha declared so emphatically that en-couragement in doing good and discouragement from doing evil deeds was one of the most important characteristics of a true friend, and for the same reason the great philosophers and moralists of classical antiquity maintained that since virtue was the basis of friendship it was a relation which could subsist only between virtuous persons, friendship without nobility of character, purity of motive, and unfailing mutual helpfulness in all the vicissitudes of life being hardly deserving of the name.

All desire the good, but few understand in what the good consists, with the paradoxical consequence that the vast majority of people spend the whole of their lives in breathless pursuit of things which they do not really want. But one who is so fortunate as to find a friend who not only understands what is truly good, but who tries to realize it himself and to persuade others to realize it, discovers at the same time that by renouncing his own will, by giving up his egoistic desires for the apparent goods of the world, for the sake of doing what his friend wishes him to do, he loses his own ignorant will and gains in its stead an enlightened will – a will set on that which in his inmost being he really desires – and realizes that in bondage to the will of a virtuous friend resides the secret of perfect spiritual freedom. The ideal of 'the good friend' (*kalyāna mitra*) in the ordinary social acceptation of the term now passes over into that of 'the good friend' in an exalted spiritual sense, for the difference between the two is not one of kind but only of degree. As his understanding of what is ethically good in the everyday affairs of human life deepens into an understanding of what is spiritually desirable in the more complex issues confronting the soul, as his comprehension of truth ranges with wider and ever wider sweep from the particular to the universal, the mundane to the supramundane, Samsāra to Nirvāna, the good friend becomes by insensible degrees the trusted counsellor, the trusted counsellor the spiritual guide or guru, the guru the Bodhisattva, and the Bodhisattva the Buddha, just as among the colours of the rainbow red merges imperceptibly into orange, orange into yellow, yellow into green, and so on. The Buddha is described in the Scriptures as the Good Friend, as the Elder Brother of Mankind; and such He indeed is in the highest sense of these words. For His love (*maitrī*) for all sentient beings, His understanding (*prajñā*) of in what consists their highest good, and His resolve (*praṇidhāna*) to help them in every possible way to realize it, are not limited and contingent in character like those exhibited by mundane friends but, on the contrary, unlimited and absolute.

'As above so below.' By virtue of the indispensable element of self-negation which it involves, the relation of friendship is able to symbolize in human and social form the submission of the will of the disciple to that of the guru, just as this relation in its turn is for the same reason able to symbolize the annihilation of the individual in the cosmic will, the joyous submission of the soul to the moral and spiritual order of the universe. Similarly, the selfless affection which we feel for an ordinary friend is symbolical of the devotion with which we regard the Good Friend of humanity, the Buddha; for just as it is out of affection for our friend that we do his will rather than our own, so it is out of devotion to the Buddha that we give up our ignorant and egoistic will in order to conform ourselves to His enlightened and selfless will as expressed in the Dharma which He taught. Friendship is thus of the profoundest possible significance. Through it we perceive 'as in a glass darkly' the pure and tranquil lineaments of Enlightenment itself. It affords us yet another example of the symbolic nature of human relationships, of the sacramental character of life itself, teaching that spiritual insight does not consist in seeing new sights with the old eyes but in seeing the old sights with new eyes, just as 'religious' life is not so much a different kind of life as the same old life lived in a new way. We discover the emotional equivalents of spiritual truths by perceiving the spiritual significance of our ordinary emotional experiences. By learning to see our good friend as the Buddha we are eventually able to discover the Buddha as our

Good Friend, and by accustoming ourselves to prefer the will of another to our own we are able gradually to prepare ourselves for that utter annihilation of egoistic will in the Dharma of Selflessness which is the essence of Enlightenment.

The Middle Way

That 'the leaves return to the root' is true not only in a natural but also in a supernatural sense. There seems to be a universal law in accordance with which, as though in a ceaseless backward-circling movement, the most complex and exalted forms of life continue to keep in touch with the simpler and more familiar forms from which they sprang. The apex of the pyramid of consciousness, though towering aloft above its base, yet stands, indeed must stand, squarely upon it. Thus it is that man, in his ascent from the spatio-temporal life of the senses and intellect to the non-spatial and non-temporal life of the spirit, not only does not leave the life of the senses entirely behind him, but in fact gathers it up into and enfolds it with the life of the spirit, illuminating it as it were from within, and transforming the mundane appearance into the sign and symbol, even into a tolerably adequate expression, of transcendental Reality. He depicts his experiences in the sphere of the Formless by means of shapes and colours derived from his experiences in the world of form, giving to airy nothing (as it must ever appear to those who have no knowledge or experience of it) if not a local habitation and a name, at least a recognizable sign and provisional designation.

This is true not only of each experience taken individually, but also of the totality of experiences which together comprise the entire grand sweep of the normative life. Although essentially supra-temporal they have been represented as unfolding as a series within time, and man's gradual achievement of them spoken of as though it consisted in a progress in a straight line along the successive stages of a path. In most of the great religious traditions of the world, particularly in that which derives from the Enlightenment of the Buddha and which we designate as Buddhism, this symbol of the Path or Way is repeated with every conceivable variation. Sometimes it appears as a path of ascent from lower to higher grades of phenomenal existence, sometimes as a path of gradual self-purification from the stains of desire, anger, and ignorance. Sometimes, again, it is spoken of as an inward-going as distinguished from an outward-going path or way, and sometimes as a way of escape from the sufferings of the Saṁsāra to the imperishable bliss of Nirvāṇa. Perhaps the most important and certainly the profoundest of the innumerable variants of this protean symbol is that in which it appears as a Middle Path or Way between the various extreme positions in ethics, psychology, and metaphysics.

If in the sphere of social relations familiarity breeds contempt, in the world of religious symbolism it is as apt to generate its opposite, namely idolatry; which is at bottom nothing but the substitution of the symbol for the thing symbolized, the taking of the more or less arbitrary designation (useful enough, indeed, for practical purposes) as the accurate and adequate description of Reality. This kind of error is particularly liable to occur with regard to all those spatio-temporal symbols by means of which the trans-spatial and supra-temporal experiences of the spiritual life are described, so that it is almost impossible to avoid thinking of them as actually conditioned by the forms of space and time. Such, indeed, are the limitations of thought and speech, and so ineffaceably do they retain the lineaments of their sensuous ancestry, that even when we wish to emphasize the non-spatial and non-temporal character of our spiritual life we can do little better than assert, with more or less latinity, that it is 'outside' space or that it 'transcends' the temporal series, thus perpetuating the error by our very effort to destroy it.

When, therefore, we speak of the *Mādhyama Mārga*, the Middle Way, of Buddhism, as lying between the two extremes of self-indulgence and self-mortification, or eternalism and annihilationism, it is only too easy to picture it as stretching between them in a strictly material and spatial sense, just as a road may be said to wind between two hills. From this literal and concrete way of understanding the symbol of the Path flow consequences which are spiritually disastrous. Since the road runs straight between the two hills, turning neither left nor right, the path of the spiritual life is, analogously, interpreted as a compromise, and the Golden Mean thought of as a kind of alloy of the iron of one extreme and the brass of the other in equal proportions. The assumption on which this misunderstanding is based is that both extremes are real, and that the state of consciousness to which they are presented is therefore ultimate, whereas the Buddha's teaching is from beginning to end nothing but one tremendous affirmation of the fact that the state of consciousness in which things appear as separate and mutually exclusive realities belongs to the world of illusion, and that the state of consciousness in which they flow into and interpenetrate each other alone belongs to the Realm of Truth. Following the Middle Way involves neither moral compromise nor intellectual eclecticism. The Buddha's Robe of Non-Duality is not a mere patchwork of the opposites. The only way in which we can really go 'between' the extremes is by rising 'above' them, although this expression also, being essentially spatial, may, if taken too literally, be as prolific of misunderstandings as the other.

Any attempt to deal with the 'pairs of opposites' on the level of experience at which they arrive inevitably confronts the mind with an insurmountable wall of contradiction. Over, under, across, or even through this wall it is possible to pass only by projecting oneself into a fourth dimension, as it were, in which the wall simply ceases to exist. This is, albeit in modern dress, nothing but the old Zen conundrum of how to get the goose out of the bottle without either smashing the bottle or injuring the bird. On its own level the problem is insoluble. It can be solved only by rising to a level of consciousness at which the pair of terms on which the whole problem revolves do not exist; or rather, where they are no longer contradictory or antagonistic to each other.

Reality is ineffable. Words and concepts cannot define the nature of True Suchness, but serve simply to designate it for practical purposes. Those who are still in bondage to ignorance do not, however, realize this, and regard the innumerable pairs of opposites which the polarizing activity of their discriminating mind superimposes on the pure Voidness as realities. Having discriminated things as good and evil, pleasant and painful, mine and thine, *et cetera*, the deluded individual pursues the former and rejects the latter. The flames of desire and hatred spring up and rage as fiercely as a forest-fire, while in their wake the pangs of disappointment, frustration, and despair follow in inevitable sequence. Buddhism lays the axe of Wisdom at the very root of the tree of mundane existence. It points out that if suffering is the bitter fruit, pleasure the fragrant flowers, desires the thick branches, and ignorance the sturdy trunk of that tree, then the mutually antagonistic concepts of ego and non-ego, together with their numerous little derivative pairs of opposites, are the tough and tangled major and minor roots thereof.

To follow the Middle Way means to transcend the conceptual activity of the discriminating mind and to achieve that state of consciousness in which things no longer stand over against each other as mutually exclusive entities, but wherein they exist in a state of 'unimpeded mutual solution', each interpenetrating all, and all interpenetrating each. This supreme status of consciousness, this ultimate abode of Reality, is designated as Śūnyatā, the entire emptiness or voidness of all conceptual activity, of all separate existence, of all pain and suffering. It is also designated as *tathatā*, Suchness, and *bodhi*, Enlightenment; and One Who has attained Thereto is known as a Tathāgata, as a Buddha. The path to that attainment is the Middle Way, the treading of which means not the fainthearted evasion of the contradictions inherent in human life (which is, ultimately, nothing but a subjective mental condition objectified) but the unremitting endeavour to resolve them by reflecting on their essential voidness and by rising to a state of consciousness in which they as such no longer occur. It is for this reason that a great Mahāyāna teacher has gone as far as to declare the *Mādhyama Mārga*, the Middle Way, to be in principle identical with Śūnyatā, the Voidness – which is the last word uttered by Buddhism before it passes beyond the boundaries of thought and speech to lose itself in the silence of the 'Ineffable'.

WHOLENESS AND HOLINESS

HUMAN PERSONALITY IS NOT SIMPLE BUT COMPOUND. This does not mean, however, that the 'parts' of which it is said to be 'composed' are in reality exterior to each other, or that they lie side by side like marbles in a box or peas in a pod. The elements of which it is made up merge into each other by imperceptible degrees, like the colours of the rainbow, so that we are unable to tell where one ends and the other begins. Now blending into unity, now flashing forth into diversity, thought, emotion, and action change and interchange like the iridescent green and gold and purple of a pigeon's neck. No thought is so remote, no concept so abstract, that it fails to be tinged, however lightly and delicately it may be, with the hue of some emotion proper to the person by whom it was conceived. Similarly, no emotion, however impetuous or 'thoughtless' from the mode of its outward expression it may be inferred to be, can arise without that element of cognitive activity which, by discriminating the object of an emotion, at the same time constitutes the very possibility of its existence. That action is in the same way inextricably interfused with both thought and emotion – being as it were pulled by the one from without and pushed by the other from within – and that all three are interpenetrated by the will, requires only to be stated in order to be at once understood.

But in spite of this interfusion of the so-called elements or aspects of human personality it is nevertheless a fact that the will is logically prior to thought, emotion, and action; that if they are the green and gold and purple of the pigeon's neck, it is the neck itself. Consequently, any traditional discipline or way of life which aims at effecting a radical change or complete transformation of the total human personality pursues through all the bewildering complexity of its methods the single objective of turning the will in a direction diametrically opposite to that in which it normally proceeds. It seeks, in other words, to make it negate the sense of separative selfhood instead of affirming it, to interpenetrate rather than to exclude. The whole process of the religious, spiritual, or normative life is essentially nothing but a progressive attenuation of the ego-sense, and any particular observance or practice, regardless of how 'sacred' or 'profane' it may outwardly seem, is to be judged useful in so far as it subserves, and useless and even positively harmful in so far as it does not subserve, this process of attenuation.

Just as the jewelled brilliance of the pigeon's iridescent neck flashes, when turned suddenly towards the sun, with an unimaginable wealth of ever-changing hues, such as were never dreamed of when it glittered dully in the shade, – so does the personality wherein the will has negated all sense of separative selfhood – turning away from the sharp outlines and dense shadows of the world of forms to bathe itself in the soft golden splendour of the shadowless Clear Light of the Void – dart forth through its cognitive aspect the pure crimson ray of Wisdom (*prajñā*), through its emotional aspect the dazzling white radiance of Compassion (*karuṇā*), and through its dynamic aspect the rich blue light of Skilful Activity (*upāya*). Whereas the will which on the contrary affirms the sense of separative selfhood expresses itself through the cognitive, emotional, and dynamic aspects of the personality which it ensouls as the darkness of delusion, the blotchy green and brown of lust-and-hatred, and the gloomy purple of violence, respectively. Only a personality which is egoless within can manifest the triple egolessness of thought, emotion, and action without.

But since everything in the universe not only interpenetrates, but also is interpenetrated by, every other thing, the will not only acts upon and modifies thought, emotion, and action, but is at the same time acted upon and modified by each of them. So that although the secret of spiritual practice does indeed reside in the transformation or redirection of the will from self-affirmation to self-negation, this transformation or redirection may be effected indirectly by transforming or redirecting its cognitive, emotional, and active instruments. For although the will, thought, emotion, and action are distinguishable from each other they are not divisible, so that to modify the shape or direction, as it were, of any one of them is simultaneously to modify the shape and direction of the rest. In any given personality one aspect does, indeed, normally predominate, and to modify the will by modifying this aspect is for that personality the simplest and most natural way of achieving the complete negation of the sense of separative selfhood. Hence the three paths of Wisdom, Devotion, and Service which unfold within the One Way of self-emptying or self-negation. It should not be thought, however, that when an aspirant follows any one of these paths and reaches the Goal, which is the realization that all things are void of separative selfhood, he reaches it by means of transformed and redirected thought, emotion, or action taken by itself. Although any aspect of personality may be used as the fulcrum on which is rested the lever of spiritual practice, nevertheless, since personality is an indivisible whole, all its aspects are elevated simultaneously. Moreover, not only does thought, for example, work upon emotion directly, but indirectly too; for by transforming thought the will is transformed, and the transformed will in turn works upon thought, emotion, and activity, manifesting through them with a steadily increasing intensity of Wisdom, Compassion, and Skilful Activity, as we have already seen. Therefore one who follows the path of Wisdom will increase in *karuṇā*, and one who follows the path of devotion will grow in *prajñā*. Ultimately, every spiritual aspirant has sedulously to cultivate each aspect of his personality, neglecting none, even though he is free (logically, if not psychologically) to choose any one of them as a starting-point, and even though any one of them may predominate in his personality and therefore determine the principal method which he employs to reach the goal.

Among such methods that of symbolical personification frequently occurs. Not only is it possible for the spiritual aspirant to visualize the Voidness as the glorified and transfigured personality radiating Wisdom, Love, and Power at white heat as it were, but it is also possible for him to conceive each of these aspects separately as an independent personality, one the manifestation of infinite Wisdom, one of boundless Compassion, and one of Energy unlimited. Each of these aspects may be divided and subdivided endlessly, thus multiplying the forms of Voidness to the point at which they can be correlated with the number of paths followed by the different classes of devotees. And just as all particular paths are comprehended within the One Path, which is at the same time the Great Way (*Mahāyāna*) and the Middle Way (*Mādhyama Mārga*), so are all personalities embraced by the One Personality, variously known as the 'Universal' (*Sambhogakāya*), 'Meditation' (*Dhyāni*), or 'Primordial' (*Ādi*) Buddha. The three aspects of this One Supreme Personality are individualized as the three principal Bodhisattvas of the Tibetan 'pantheon', Mañjuśrī representing the Wisdom of the Buddha, Avalokiteśvara His Compassion, and Vajrapāṇi his Energy. It is therefore possible for the spiritual practice of any given aspirant not only to take the form of the cultivation of a particular aspect of his own personality, or the development of a particular quality, whether of the will, thought, emotion, or activity; but it is also possible for it to assume the form of devotion to a particular personification of the Void, regardless of whether this personification comprises all four aspects or consists of only one of them. To worship Mañjuśrī means to develop Wisdom, on the principle that we assimilate, or are assimilated to, the nature of that about which we constantly think. Similarly, the sādhana of Avalokiteśvara or Vajrapāṇi may be equated with the transformation of lust and hatred into Compassion, or with the raising of action to the status of Skilful Means.

Yet does it remain imperatively necessary for the devotee to understand that at the same time he worships indirectly, through the medium of the direct object of his devotion, all other objects of devotion whatsoever. For, as already said, the various aspects of human personality to which these ideal beings pertain are inextricably interfused, so that each interpenetrates, and is simultaneously interpenetrated by, every other, thus exemplifying microcosmically the macrocosmic truth that

Nothing in the world is single;
All things, by a law divine,
In one another's being mingle,...

Strange as it may seem, the devotee of Mañjuśrī indirectly worships Avalokiteśvara, and *vice versa*; the devotee of the Buddha indirectly worships Christ, while the devotee of Christ is (blasphemous as the thought might to him appear) all unknowingly worshipping the Buddha. The recognition of this fact on the plane of personified ideals contributes largely to the adoption of a tolerant attitude of mind; while to recognize it on the level of intellectual, emotional, and kinetic development does not merely contribute, but is even indispensably necessary, to the full and perfect unfolding of the flower of human personality. It is assuredly more than an accident of etymology that the words 'wholeness' and 'holiness' originate from the same root. Holiness is nothing but wholeness at the very highest possible level of experience. Spiritual life consists not in the development of any one aspect of human personality alone, however prominent or important that may be, but in the harmonious unfoldment of all of them as expressions of its entire emptiness of all separate selfhood. It is impossible for thought, emotion, or activity to fall outside the scope of any comprehensive scheme of spiritual culture. Even though we may for the time being concentrate on the cultivation of one particular aspect of our personality, on the development of a single quality; even though it may be necessary for us to begin with the worship of one particular Ideal, in the end we have to follow the advice of Milarepa, who says:

> *Gurus, Devas, Ḍākinīs –*
> *Combine these in a single whole and worship that;*
> *The goal of aspiration, the meditation, and the practice –*
> *Combine these in a single whole, and gain Experiential*
>   *Knowledge;*
> *This life, the next life, and the life between [in Bar-do] –*
> *Regard these all as one, and make thyself accustomed to them*
>   *[thus as one]*

Desire for the Eternal

Whether it be true or not that it was at the flaming forth of Cosmic Desire that the universe sprang into being, it is nevertheless true that it is due to the propulsive power of their desires that men and women are precipitated again and again into bodily existence. The different aspects of the average human personality can, in fact, be considered as the various deformations of the one central craving for separate individuality, and the whole course of human life may be interpreted as a series of attempts to satisfy one desire or another. Although the possibility of gratifying any given desire varies in accordance with the circumstances which surround it, the modern psychology of the West is emphatic that its conscious or unconscious suppression, particularly when it occurs in the form of sexual desire, is not only painful but even positively harmful. The stronger the desire, and the more forcible the method of its suppression, the more violent is the shock of its recoil upon the psyche, and the more disastrous the consequent disruption of personality. Modern Western psychology therefore sees in the suppression of desire the solution to the problem of human suffering, and in its satisfaction the key to happiness.

This is all quite true so far as it goes, but it does not, unfortunately, go nearly far enough. The facts are not all the facts, and the truth is therefore not the whole truth. For while it is undoubtedly true that man is a bundle of desires, it is certainly not true that those desires are for the gross pleasures of the senses, or even for the comparatively refined pleasures of the mind, exclusively. Man thirsts for the dews of heaven no less keenly than he hungers for the bread of earth. The mistake of the mere psychologists consists in their being incapable of recognizing fully the inexhaustible richness of the potentialities of the human heart, which mirrors Enlightenment no less than ignorance, and bears in its unfathomable depths the reflection of the stars of heaven no less than of the glow-worms of the earth. They refuse to recognize that we have immortal longings in us as well as transitory desires and that the denial of the one may have as devastating an effect upon the integrity of personality as the suppression of the other. Modern Western man and his Eastern imitators are miserable not because they have frustrated the cravings of their bodies, but because they have denied the aspirations of their souls. They will be able to achieve the peace of wholeness only when they recognize that although the potentialities of the human heart are infinite, only one of them is to be actualized; that although the reflections which it contains are numberless, the reflection of Enlightenment is brighter and clearer than all others, – just as the moon, by reason of its superior luminosity, is reflected more brightly and clearly in the waters of the lake than are the stars; and that although desires are multitudinous, the Desire for the Eternal is basic to them all, so that whatever else finds satisfaction, if this finds not satisfaction the result is frustration and misery.

Desire for the transitory is doomed, sooner or later, to disappointment. Even if it is possible to strive after and obtain such an object of desire, it is not possible to grasp hold of it for ever. Only in the Desire for the Eternal resides the possibility of permanent satisfaction and everlasting joy. For the Eternal gives itself freely to those who freely give themselves to it. All unillumined desire is really a groping in the dark for Enlightenment, a looking for Buddhahood in the wrong direction, as it were, so that even when we succeed in gaining the object of an unillumined desire we do not feel satisfied, because we were really not looking for that at all, but for something else. For this reason, also, when the Desire for the Eternal is satisfied, all other desires are satisfied simultaneously, since they were nothing but deformations of it. This is the meaning of the saying that if we seek first the Kingdom of Heaven, all things will be added unto us; although we should, of course, seek the Kingdom of Heaven for its own sake, and not for the sake of what, it is promised, will be added unto us if we do so. Otherwise we shall succeed in gaining neither the Kingdom of Heaven nor anything else. Modern Western man must once again recognize himself as an essentially spiritual being, and acknowledge the attainment of Enlightenment as the Supreme End of human life. Otherwise he will continue to whirl round and round in the vortex of existence, ignorant, frustrated, and miserable.

ENLIGHTENMENT

THE HISTORICAL FACT of the Buddha's Enlightenment beneath the Bodhi Tree at Bodh Gaya is the alpha and omega, the beginning and the end, of the entire system of Buddhism. It is the beginning inasmuch as the Dharma taught by the Buddha is not the product of mere unillumined mental activity, a philosophical system in the mundane sense of the term to be accepted or rejected at will, but a transcription into conceptual symbols of His own truly ineffable inner experience of Reality. Nor was this transcription made with the slightest intention of gratifying idle, albeit philosophically camouflaged, curiosity, but with the sole object of affording adequate practical guidance to whomsoever, possessed of faith, were desirous of treading in the footsteps of the Buddha and obtaining Enlightenment for themselves even as He had obtained it for Himself. It is in this sense that Enlightenment is to be regarded as the end, the final term, of the Buddha Dharma. We take refuge in the Buddha believing that He was Himself Fully Enlightened; in the Dharma, with the conviction that as the expression of His Enlightenment in conceptual terms, it is capable of guiding us thereto; and in the Sangha, confident that as the living embodiment of the Tradition they are capable both of expounding it theoretically by their teachings and exemplifying it practically in their lives.

It therefore follows that any attempt to elucidate Buddhist doctrines which is not based upon the full acceptance of the root reality of the Buddha's Enlightenment, with all the momentous consequences which stem therefrom, is wholly unacceptable to any believing and practising Buddhist and moreover foredoomed from the beginning to miserable failure, leaving out as it does the one supreme and all-explaining Fact whence the whole system issues and into which it finally returns. From this fatal omission arises the whole sticky web of 'contradictions' and 'difficulties' which the profane academic mind delights to elaborate spider-like from the abysm of its own learned ignorance and wherein the unwary student becomes speedily entrapped. The Buddha was not an agnostic, a social reformer, a humanitarian, nor anything else to be adequately described by attaching to it any such fashionable label, but simply a man who had by His own efforts become Buddha, the Enlightened One. Those who are for any reason unable to accept Him as such had better leave Him and His religion strictly alone, since however learned they may be they will never be able to understand more than the superficialities of either. A Sinhalese peasant or a Tibetan muleteer has a better chance of comprehension than they. For the feet of the devotee are upon the Path, however short the distance they have traversed, and their eyes have caught a glimpse of the Goal, from however far away they may have beheld a beam of its splendour.

The academic approach to Buddhism is not simply neutral with regard to the possibility of Enlightenment, despite all its protestations of objectivity and impartiality, but in fact definitely hostile to it, since what it really endeavours to do is to judge the Wisdom of the Buddha in accordance with the perverted standards of its own unillumined and deluded mentality, thereby seeking to subordinate Knowledge to ignorance, and striving to drag Egolessness down to the level of egoism. We are not to shape Buddhism in accordance with our understanding of it, but to mould our understanding in accordance with Buddhism. Otherwise instead of taking refuge in the Buddha, the Dharma, and the Sangha we should be expecting them to take refuge in us! Such is the difference between the attitude of the devout, however unscholarly, and that of the undevout, however scholarly.

Such an inversion of the legitimate hierarchy of things, wherein Enlightenment occupies the topmost position, and wherein all other varieties of knowledge and experience are ranged in higher or lower degrees in accordance with the extent to which they conduce or do not conduce to its attainment, is characteristic of the present age, when things sacred are subordinated to things profane, and when the worldling, with all his ignorance and desires, dares to sit in judgement on the Wisdom of Buddhas and Bodhisattvas. In the same way, the rare gift of human life is regarded not as the supreme opportunity for attaining Enlightenment, but as a spark of pleasure flashing momentarily between the terminals of two eternities of non-existence. Hence the mad competitive rush for the possession of worldly goods, for the acquisition of wealth and power, which we see before our eyes in the world today. Hence the wars and rumours of wars which spread like some stygian smoke across the face of the earth.

> *Turning and turning in the widening gyre*
> *The falcon cannot hear the falconer;*
> *Things fall apart; the centre cannot hold ...*

although it is not so much that the Centre – Enlightenment – cannot hold on to the circumference, as that the circumference has lost its grip on the Centre. The falcon cannot hear the falconer, but the converse is not true.

Enlightenment persists as a permanent possibility at the heart of every living being, however long the actualization of it may be delayed; just as the disc of the moon continues to be reflected in the waters of the ocean, however broken and distorted by the agitation of the waves its image may be. Only when the falcon learns to hear the voice of the falconer, when the circumference of our lives stands in correct relation to its Centre, when the traditional hierarchy of values is restored, and Enlightenment once more recognized as the crown and consummation of human endeavour, will things fall together again instead of apart, and peace and harmony reign in the outer even as in the inner life of man.

THE PARABLE OF THE RAFT

TO ELIMINATE THE SENSE OF SEPARATIVE SELFHOOD is the first and last duty of one who sincerely desires to lead the genuine Buddhist life. The serpent of egoism must be uncoiled ring by ring from the heart, its twin fangs of greed and malice extracted, its deadly venom neutralized drop by drop. Yet it should not for one moment be supposed that the spiritual life is for this reason one of abstention only. The terms used to describe it may indeed be negative in form, but since they refer to a delusion which is itself in the strictest sense a negation (being in fact a dichotomization, and therefore a limitation, of the wholeness of existence) they are in principle affirmative, in accordance with the canon that two negations constitute an affirmation. The positive albeit symbolical complement of the doctrine of no-selfhood is that of the perfect mutual interpenetration of all the seemingly discrete 'things' of which the universe is composed, all from the highest to the lowest being reflected, as it were, in each, and each in all. Since Buddhahood also, like any other supposedly individual thing, comes to be reflected in this way, it follows that it not only transcends the aspirant from without as the ultimate goal of his quest, but also exists within him immanently as the impulse behind all his endeavours to reach it. Buddhism asserts that the Buddha-nature exists potentially not only in every human being, but even in every non-human being, in every stock and stone, in every tree and flower and blade of grass that is. From the embrace of its boundless compassion even the dust motes are not excluded. Much less still does it exclude a single human creature, or deny the possibility of enlightenment to any form of life, for how many births soever ignorance and desire may delay the actualization of that exalted potentiality.

The Dharma is simply the means which the Buddha, the Enlightened One, provided for enabling us to awake to the reality of our own dormant Buddha-nature. It is like the push given to a sleeping man. Whether we think of it in terms of moral practice, of concentration and meditation, or even of intuitive wisdom (the three ascending stages into which the Path is divided), it is never to be regarded as an end in itself, but only as a means to an end, nor as valuable or significant for its own sake, but only for the sake of the efficacy with which it conduces to Enlightenment. 'Using the figure of a raft, brethren, will I teach you the Dharma, as something to leave behind, not to take with you,' declared the Buddha. Just as it would be ridiculous for a man who had succeeded, with the help of raft or boat, in crossing a raging torrent and landing safely on the further shore, to load it on to his shoulders and, out of a sense of gratitude, bear it with him wherever he went, so would it be foolish for one who had crossed over the stormy waters of the stream of birth-and-death to the Further Shore of Nirvāṇa not to give up the Dharma after it was no longer of use to him. The moral of this parable applies with equal force to the Dharma as a whole and to every one of the limbs of which it is composed, to each successive stage of the spiritual life no less than to the Path in its entirety. Moral observance or object of meditation, ritual act or philosophical doctrine, are helps when utilized with the understanding that they are nothing more than means to one supreme end, which is Enlightenment, and hindrances when viewed and valued as ends in themselves. The suitability of any given means (for the question of its truth or untruth cannot arise) depends solely upon the extent to which it is adapted to the character of the particular aspirant for whom it is intended. Since character and temperament vary not only from individual to individual, but also from one race and one age, one continent and one culture to another, every geographical expansion of the Dharma will call for a corresponding extension of the range of its means, each new conquest demand a fresh adaptation. Enlightenment is thus the one constant factor in the history of Buddhism, and it is the presence or absence of enlightened persons among them that ultimately determines whether any sect or school has succeeded in transmitting through the ages the enlivening spirit of the Buddha's Doctrine, as distinct from merely preserving the dead letter of it in books.

One might think that these statements would be clear and incontestable enough in the eyes of those who had a superficial acquaintance, even, with the contents of the scriptures; that having, as followers of the Buddha, accepted Enlightenment as their ultimate goal, they could hardly fail to understand that the Dharma was simply the means of attaining that supreme end, or help appreciating the fact that it might be necessary for this means to be adapted from place to place and from time to time, in accordance with the widely varying temperaments of different classes of aspirants. But such is, unfortunately, not always the case. Those are not wanting who, despite the fact that their own 'shrunken and aberrant' form of Buddhism has been for centuries unable to produce even a single Arahant, clamorously insist that they alone possess what they are pleased to call 'the Pure Dharma', and that all other forms of Buddhism whatsoever are 'degenerations' of the primitive and authentic teaching. Such an attitude smacks far more strongly of insular prejudice and Protestant 'fundamentalism' (wherein lies, perchance, its true origin) than of the Dharma of the All-Enlightened and All-Compassionate One. If the plight of those who, after crossing over to the further shore, shoulder their raft and carry it about with them, is ridiculous, how much more ridiculous is the spectacle of those foolish ones who, clutching to their bosoms a broken fragment of the raft that has been provided for their use, strut proudly up and down the banks of the hither shore, and hurl abuse at those who, in vessels constructed on the same principle, but of slightly different pattern, are engaged in actually ferrying across the swollen waters to the further shore! And how much more ridiculous still do such people appear when they proclaim, as they have in fact proclaimed from the temple tops more than once of late, that they alone are the true sailors and that all others (clapping their hands impatiently to their eyes) are either not sailors or have run aground on the mud-flats of the hither shore! If those who had crossed over, or who were crossing over, the stream, could spare time for a backward glance at the antics of these self-styled sailors, they might reply to them, with a smile of compassion, in the Buddha's own words:

They who cross the Ocean's deeps
Make a bridge and leave the swamps.
Other folk tie reeds together:
But the wise have crossed the stream.

THE AWAKENING OF THE HEART

DEEP IN THE MUD AND SLIME of the river bed lodges the lotus seed. In the cold green darkness of that nether world of waters it dwells unseen and unsuspected. Age after age it seems to lurk there under layers of rotted vegetation and soft black mud, while the abysmal silence broods mother-like above it and all round, holding it tenderly in the soft darkness of her womb. Then, one day, a shaft of light comes plunging down through the watery gloom like a sword of emerald fire. The darkness seems to heave, shudder, and thrill beneath its touch. That twilight world glows a pale and delicate green, then a misty amber, and at last a clear bright translucent gold. With the light comes fire. And the seed, the lotus seed down there in its dark bed of death, feels the light and the warmth of that inflowing life and struggles to respond. Slowly, slowly come forth the thin white filaments, the pale green stem, the tiny tender leaves, and at last, just as the plant thrusts itself up from the chill green water into the warm sunlit air, comes forth all virgin-hard and tightly wrapped up within itself a little bud. But as the heat of the sun waxes stronger the bud swells and slowly unfolds until its pure white petals and golden heart are wide open to receive the kiss of benediction from its Lord.

By means of such a simile as this have the Buddhist teachers of old endeavoured to illustrate the gradual awakening of Wisdom and Compassion within the human heart. They emphasize that the seed of it – elsewhere symbolized as the gem (*maṇi*) which is within the lotus (*padma*) of sentient existence – is there all the time, however deeply and darkly it may be hidden away beneath layer on layer of greed, hatred, and delusion. For since everything in the universe reflects, and is in turn reflected by, every other thing, the Buddha-Nature is mirrored in the depths not only of every human heart but in every grain of dust and blade of grass that is. As Aśvaghoṣa says, everything is perfumed with the fragrance of True Suchness. Even the meanest and vilest of things enshrines immaculately within itself the Jewel of Enlightenment, of Buddhahood. The slumbering seed is stirred into wakefulness by the light and warmth of that energic Wisdom-Compassion, that bright effluence of the essence of Reality, of Voidness, which is personified as the Bodhisattva, as the Universal Buddha, or as Amitābha. For just as Enlightenment is reflected in our ignorance and suffering, so also are the ignorance and suffering of all sentient beings reflected in Enlightenment, so that the Bodhisattva is unable to cease from his selfless labours so long as even one grain of dust remains undelivered. It is in the interaction of Enlightenment-reflecting ignorance and ignorance-reflecting Enlightenment that the possibility of human salvation or emancipation consists. It is for this reason that the Buddha said that we should take refuge both in ourself (because the Bodhicitta, the reflection of Enlightenment, is there), and in the Dharma (because it is the means of salvation which the Compassion of all the Buddhas and Bodhisattvas offers in response to the reflection of our ignorance in their Enlightenment). Religion and the spiritual life are therefore built into the very structure of Reality – if such a stiff and architectural metaphor is permissible with reference to That which is essentially dynamic. They are no mere grafts on to the Tree of Life but spring from it as its fairest blossom and ripest fruit. The appearance of Buddhas and Bodhisattvas in this and other worlds, their preaching of the Doctrine of Universal Enlightenment and Salvation, their founding of the great Brotherhood of love and service are, therefore, not simply accidents of history but, given the nature of Reality as conceived by Buddhist philosophy, the inevitable expression of the inmost essence of existence.

Such also is the activity of one who sincerely and selflessly consecrates himself to the propagation of the Buddha's Word. By endeavouring to reflect more and more perfectly the Wisdom of the Buddha he automatically reflects His Compassion also, for the two are one – the intellectual and emotional expressions respectively of the Plenum-Voidness of the perfect mutual interpenetration of all things. We preach the Buddha's Word because we cannot help so doing. Not with any arrogant assumption of superiority over those to whom we preach, not as the result of any conclusion reached by processes purely intellectual, but simply because the Light which has awakened the lotus seed within our hearts into the bloom of full or partial Enlightenment cannot rest there, but refracts from it in all directions on to the millions of other lotus seeds which are still buried deep down in the mud of greed, hatred, and delusion. From every one of these seeds, from the heart of every sentient being, the White Lotus of Supreme Enlightenment, the fragrance whereof is Compassion Universal, will, sooner or later, spring forth. This belief is not only the foundation of Buddhism as a practical religion, but the *raison d'être* of the unrivalled tradition of Buddhist tolerance as well. The preacher of Buddhism sees mankind not as a string of sinners and heretics dancing along the road to hell, but as of old the Eye of the Buddha saw them – as a bed of lotuses in the various stages of their upward growth, some still immersed in the slime, others partly out of it, but all of them needing only the light and warmth of Compassion to awaken the hard green bud of their hearts into the full bloom of Perfect Enlightenment. For this reason he seeks not merely to indoctrinate, much less still does he ever condemn, but with the aspiration simply to awaken with the life-kindling touch of Buddha's Teaching – exhibited in his practice as well as in his preaching – that small seed of Enlightenment which, he knows, sleeps within the mire and darkness of every human heart irrespective of sex, social position, race, and religion, he lives and moves and has his radiant being in the midst of the cold green darkness of separative lives and forms seeking simply to love. For he knows that only Love and Compassion are able to lead, one day, to that Awakening of the Heart which is the goal of religion and the highest fulfilment of human life.

THE SIMPLE LIFE

MEN AND WOMEN BEWILDERED by the ever-increasing complexity of modern civilization cry out for the simple life as a drowning man gasps for air. Visions of cool trees and quiet cottages arise before eyes almost blinded by the glare of neon lights; and ears well nigh deaf with the thunder of traffic and shriek of machinery seem to catch, during brief interludes of silence, the sound of white surf as it sweeps hissing up the beach or the song of a bird as it floats sweet and clear through the moonlight from the darkness of distant trees.

But the simple life is by no means one of ease and idleness, as the town-dweller, with his sentimental 'idealization' of life in the country, is apt to suppose. Nor is it necessarily associated with lonely hermitages wreathed in mountain mist or gleaming coral beaches fringed with languorous palms, although the relative freedom from 'external' distractions and irritations which such places enjoy may make them more helpful to the leading of a simple life than others less fortunate. For the simple life is also a strenuous one, being the product of a process of simplification, a reduction of life to its barest essentials; and the successful accomplishment of this process is, amidst the monstrous jungle-growth of the complexities of modern living, a task calling for unremitting endeavour and inflexible resolve. Nor does it involve merely the simplification of the external mode of one's existence, but something far more fundamental upon which hinges not only this but every other mode of existence as well.

But before we can reduce life to its essentials we must determine what those essentials are, otherwise the expression remains a mere gaudy flower of rhetoric barren of all fruition in experience. And before we can determine what are the essentials of life and what its adventitious trappings we must ask ourselves the question, essential to what? For life as we ordinarily live it is obviously not an end in itself, but only a means to an end, and until we know what that end is it is impossible for us to judge what in our lives is essential, and what inessential, to the attainment of it.

Buddhism posits *bodhi*, or the realization of Transcendent Wisdom, as the ultimate goal not only of every human being but of every other form of sentient existence as well. Life is for the sake of Enlightenment. Not even the tiniest blade of grass or most microscopic speck of dust will be excluded from that incomparable consummation, however many revolutions of the wheel of birth and death they may in the meantime have to undergo. The essentials of life are those things which are helpful to the attainment of Enlightenment, and it is back to these naked boughs that the luxuriant foliage and innumerable buds of our life-tree must be ruthlessly stripped and pruned if ever it is to bear its loveliest blossoms and most ambrosial fruit. The truly simple life is that which is dedicated solely to the attainment of Supreme Wisdom, and wherein each thought, word, and deed is integrated to the achievement of that end. Killing, stealing, wrong means of livelihood, and all other forms of unskilful bodily action must be given up until those actions alone remain the performance of which abounds in spiritual significance. Thus bodily action is simplified into Mudrā. The use of false, frivolous, abusive, and obscene speech must be gradually restricted until no word is uttered without some background of spiritual recollection behind it. Thus speech is simplified into Mantra. Greedy, malicious, and deluded thoughts must be eliminated until the concentrated mind admits only thoughts that are pure, compassionate, and illumined. Thus thought is simplified into Samādhi. As the Bodhisattva disciplines himself in this way his body, speech, and mind gradually become as it were transparent, and through each thought, word, and deed streams into the world the effulgence of Great Compassion, just as the beams of the rising sun leap through the windows of a room and disarm the darkness within. The truly simple life glows with significance, for its simplicity is not the dead simplicity of a skeleton but the living simplicity of a flower or a great work of art. The unessential has melted like mist from life and the Himalayan contours of the essential are seen towering with sublime simplicity above the petty hills and valleys of the futilities of mundane existence.

Far Eastern aesthetics make extensive use of a term which may be interpretively translated as 'aesthetic impoverishment'. This kind of art finds its highest expression in ink drawings which reveal a whole world of significance with three strokes of the brush, and tiny verses which seem almost to exhaust the possibilities of poetic expression within the compass of seven and thirty syllables, although the principle on which it is based is not peculiar to the realm of art but penetrates every phase of the life and culture of the Far Eastern peoples. In fact, it is an aesthetic application of the principle on which the simple life, in the sense of the Bodhisattva career, is founded, – the principle that the more rigorous the simplicity of the outward form the more clearly is the significance of the inner spirit revealed.

It is the presence of this parallelism which makes it possible to speak of the spiritual life as a work of art, as the greatest of all works of art, and which perhaps explains the aesthetic pleasure with which we contemplate the Bodhisattva ideal, an ideal which seems not only good and true but also incomparably beautiful. For the simple life is in fact all three, and where goodness, truth, and beauty abound happiness is of a surety not far to seek.

'Pauses' and 'Empty Spaces'

When the composer Mozart was asked what was the most important part of his music, he did not reply that melody, or harmony, or counterpoint, or even orchestration was the most important, but simply 'the pauses'.

As in the music of Mozart, so in the paintings of the Far Eastern – Chinese and Japanese – masters of the art of landscape. It is the empty spaces which are the most important parts of the picture. The vast empty spaces of sky, or snow, or water are not only themselves charged with mysterious significance as a cloud with lightning, but they somehow infuse that significance into the single blossomless branch, or tiny floating boat, or solitary human figure, which stands almost lost at the edge, or in the centre, of the huge blank expanse of paper, or faintly tinted silk.

And just as the pauses are the most important part of music, and the empty spaces the most important part of a picture, so are silence and emptiness the most important part of life. A life which consists of a frantic stream of external activities, without one moment of inward recollection, is like music which is an uninterrupted succession of sounds, or a picture which is crammed with figures: all three are not only meaningless, but positively painful.

As music is born of silence, and derives its significance therefrom; and as a painting is born of empty space, and derives its significance therefrom; so are our lives born of silence, of stillness, of quietude of spirit, and derive their significance, their distinctive flavour and individual quality, therefrom. The deeper and more frequent are those moments of interior silence and stillness wherein, transcending all sights and sounds, tastes and touches, we experience Reality as it is, the more rich in significance, the more truly meaningful, will our lives be.

It has been said that there is a silence of words, a silence of desires, and a silence of thoughts. Only when the egoistic will itself is 'silent', that is, no longer operative, will be heard the True Sound. Only when our hearts are utterly empty of all self-will shall we behold the True Form. And since this Silence and Emptiness are not states of mere negation, but dynamic and full of life, our thoughts and words and deeds, even the most insignificant, will be charged with a mysterious potency, like two or three notes of a flute sounding in the midst of a great pause in a symphony, or a few delicate twigs sketched in the corner of an else empty scroll.

Truly did a Chinese sage say that it is only because of empty space that the wheel is able to revolve, and houses to be made use of.

It is the pauses which make beautiful the music of our lives. It is the empty spaces which give richness and significance to them. And it is stillness which makes them truly useful.

AN OLD SAW RESHARPENED

THAT 'CHARITY BEGINS AT HOME' is an old saw, and like many another old saw one which has with repeated use lost much of its original sharpness. But traditional sayings such as this are after all the distillations of a vast ocean of human experience, and the precious pearl of wisdom which each one undoubtedly encloses is not the artificial product of mere intellectual culture but the rich result of age-long silence and suffering, offered to us gleaming from between the opening valves of the past and future ages. As such it perhaps merits a higher estimation, certainly a more careful and considerate appraisal, of its value, than that which in our familiarity we ordinarily bestow upon it.

Although this particular adage speaks of only one virtue, namely that of charity – perhaps in its more comely original sense of 'love' (*maitrī*) rather than in its cheerless modern connotation of the dole which riches disdainfully flings to poverty – the admonition it gives us as to where it should begin is applicable not only to the practice of charity but of every other virtue whatsoever, springing as it does from an insight into one of the most common weaknesses of human character, and an understanding of habits of thought which ultimately influence not one part only but the whole of our behaviour – shining scarlet threads which appear again and again running through the complicated web of mortal life.

This weakness, to insight into which the sharpness of the old saw was originally owing, like most human weaknesses springs from a strength, from the very disproportionateness of some endowment which, while it cannot be described as good in the spiritual sense, is at least a practically useful piece of equipment, in much the same way as a virtue carried to extremes becomes a vice, or as a flower runs exuberantly to seed out of the sheer perfection of its bloom.

Very early in the course of his existence in this world of suffering, the individual realizes that he is confronted, as was the race to which he belongs before him, with masses of phenomena staggering in their multiplicity and bewildering in the richness of their variety. With each phenomenon singly he is of course powerless to deal, whether it be with the numberlessness of the stars above his head, or the seeming infinity of the blades of grass beneath his feet. Without some means of dealing with them collectively thought would be compelled to beat the track of endless enumeration without ever being able to arrive at a conclusion, and the possibility of rational action would therefore be permanently excluded from the purview of human achievement. Only by the gradual perfection of techniques of generalization and abstraction which age-long usage has rendered so familiar that we forget how complicated and artificial the whole process really is, has it been possible for the human race, and for the individual who in the course of his development recapitulates racial history, to reduce the chaos of their impressions to a cosmos wherein, for the sake of accomplishing their purposes and fulfilling their desires, they might trace a recognizable pattern of thought and action, thus rendering possible the formation of societies, the efflorescence of culture, and ultimately the construction of the whole complicated machinery of supply and demand of which modern civilization for the most part consists.

One would hardly think that the seemingly innocent process of abstracting from one's experience certain impressions of blueness, distance, *et cetera*, generalizing them into a single idea, and connecting with that idea the sound 'sky', was in fact the primal sin by committing which we daily cast ourselves out from the paradise of the enjoyment of our own original nature, to fall headlong into the peril-fraught sea of repeated birth and death. But such is indeed the case: though it may be granted that it is not so much in the process of abstraction and generalization in itself that the root error of humanity lies, as in the habit of regarding the fictions of thought as having an independent real existence somewhere above or beyond or behind the stream of impressions wherefrom they were originally abstracted. So long as we remain undeceived by the specious claims of our own mental creations, recognizing them for no more than what in fact they are, as instruments of our own devising, as weapons of our own forging, as the various symbols of a system of conceptual shorthand, useful, nay indispensable, for the practical purposes for which they were invented, but without any basis in or congruence with Reality, – then not much harm is done, certainly no more than what would in any case have accrued from the desire and ignorance whereby the entire process was initiated. But when, forgetting that the concepts of the mind are simply instruments for the realization of certain purposes, we begin endowing them with a life of their own, and treat them as though they possessed independent existence and inherent validity, then flow forth consequences which are not only disastrous to right thinking and right living, but moreover productive of endless confusion, bewilderment, and misery.

Concepts such as 'the State', or 'Wealth', for example, are useful enough when they are treated simply as devices for enabling us to think clearly and act effectively with regard to the various problems involved in the political and economic relations between individuals and societies. They become dangerous only when we slip into the habit of thinking of them as things-in-themselves, and therefore of behaving as though they were ends-in-themselves. It would be easy to multiply examples such as these indefinitely, for every noun in the language is nothing but such a device for dealing with the multitude of our impressions, and therefore potentially an occasion of that same primal sin to which reference has already been made. Some such devices, though, are more dangerous than others. Not much harm is done by the belief that the word 'tree', for instance, represents an object possessing the attributes of greenness, tallness, *et cetera*, instead of being merely the symbol we attach to certain impressions of greenness, tallness, *et cetera*, more or less arbitrarily isolated from the general stream of impressions which are the content of sensuous experience. A belief such as this is harmful only as it participates in the general harmfulness of the habit of abstraction itself. But many other concepts are far less innocuous, and terrible indeed is the havoc which may be wrought by them, hanging as they do like a constellation of malignant stars above the destinies of individuals and nations. Surpassing all others with the evil intensity of its lustre, blasting and withering the whole earth with the dreadful incandescence of its beams, burns the baleful star of Māra, the deadliest asterism in the whole firmament of man's delusion, the belief in an *ātman*, the primordial error that the word 'self' represents an eternal, unchanging ego-entity somehow existing in or above or behind the various thoughts and feelings of which human personality is composed, instead of being merely the conventional label which, for practical purposes, we attach to the stream of our thoughts and feelings as a whole. With this ruling planet of delusion we are not, however, at present concerned, except inasmuch as by exhibiting in its direst form the danger with which these pages deal, it enables us to see in more definitive outline the essentials of the subject of our inquiry. Our business is not with the lord of the meridian of evil, but with one of those homelier stars hanging like a great drop of golden dew above the roof-tops of humanity.

Hanging above the temple-tops as well. For the danger against which the old adage warns us, its reminder that love should abound within our own doors before we go crying it up and down the streets outside, is applicable to the spiritual life no less than to the worldly. The salient characteristics of human nature after all remain unchanged despite variety of circumstances, and whether the quietness of the cloister or the conviviality of the hearth environ it, the human mind operates in ways not fundamentally dissimilar, possesses the same inherent strengths, and is subject to the same constitutional weaknesses. Indeed, since the cultivation of love or friendship or *maitrī*, in the most exalted sense of the term, may be said to pertain more strictly to the spiritual life (whether in or out of the cloister) than to any other, it is in the spiritual life that we should reasonably expect to find most strikingly exemplified not only its greatest strength, its maximum ardour and intensity, but its greatest weakness, its fundamental defect as well.

Not long ago a gentleman was introduced to us who professed, with almost every other breath he drew, that his sole mission in life was to 'serve Humanity'. He spoke several languages fluently, had read widely in both Eastern and Western philosophy and religion, was a not unpractised journalist, and above all else was quite sincere in his professions. (Sincerity, though, like most 'good' emotions, is not enough: if an insincere man is usually one who attempts to deceive others, a sincere one is only too often one who has succeeded in deceiving no one but himself.) Grandiose schemes for the regeneration of humanity, and for the amelioration of the lot of the Indian masses, together with the wildest generalizations and most impracticably altruistic sentiments imaginable,

Full of sound and fury, signifying nothing,
flowed from his lips in an unending stream. He did his best to
appear overwhelmed with work, and flew from one organization to another as a startled bird flies from tree to tree. After
meeting him twice or thrice, and having on each occasion
fruitlessly endeavoured to elicit from him an unambiguous
statement of what he truly believed and what he really was
trying to accomplish, and having always found that it was his
habit, when thus interrogated, to beat a hasty retreat behind a
cloud of the most vapid generalities possible, – much as a
lamp-scared squid disappears into the darkness of its own
effluvia, – we concluded that he had completely lost the earth-
touch of what are conventionally termed realities, and was
floundering his bewildered way through a cloud-cuckoo-land
of his own imagination, a realm of meaningless abstractions
wherein he had by that time become completely lost. We were
therefore hardly astonished when we found that none of his
schemes had ever borne fruit, and that, despite the loftiness of
his ideal of universal service, he had never succeeded in being
of practical use to a single one of his fellow men in even the most
ordinary and insignificant manner. Perpetually excited, invariably in a hurry, vapouring advice with the smuggest assumption of spiritual authority, he thrust upon our notice a striking
illustration of the fate that can befall the sincerest spiritual
aspirant, even, who forgets that he has not to love and serve
some unreal abstraction, whether 'Humanity' or any other conceptual symbol of the mind's own creation, but the concrete,
individual men and women whom we see living and working
and suffering around us every day of our lives. Useless our
aspirations to universal charity while the beggar on our door-
step remains unfed! Vainglorious jangles of words our repeti-
tion of Mettā-suttas, hypocritical posturings with an eye to

public approval our solemn, ponderous sittings for two minutes' 'mettā-radiation,' while the feelings of wife or child, friend or fellow-student, colleague or employee, are still smarting with the wound inflicted by some unkind or inconsiderate word.

The sad truth is that it is far less troublesome to indulge in ecstasies of love and admiration for some bloodless abstraction like 'Humanity,' than it is to love for one moment sincerely, unselfishly, and above all practically, even a single imperfect human being, with all his unreasonable demands, his baseless suspicions, his little misunderstandings and petty jealousies. This should not be understood as a general condemnation of the practice of contemplating an abstract idea, whether of love or compassion or anything else, such as may take place in certain forms of meditation. All that we are concerned to point out here is that contemplation of this kind is not an end in itself, but only a means to an end, a device whereby we are enabled to love our fellow men more truly than we could ever have done without its aid. It may be remarked that even the practice of *maitrī-bhāvana*, which is today popular with many Buddhists, according to orthodox traditions does not consist in the contemplation of the idea of *maitrī in the abstract*, but in the cultivation of the *feeling of maitrī* first of all towards the mental images of those who are nearest and dearest to us, and thereafter to those with whom our contact is merely casual and occasional, and those whom we have just seen or only heard of, in a gradually enlarging circle of affection. *Maitrī-bhāvana*, like the practice of charity, begins, or should begin, at home.

The Bodhisattva, who is born from the conjugation of the thought of universal wisdom with the feeling of boundless compassion, should not be regarded as so deeply engrossed in the thought of all the beings he will be able to save after becoming a Buddha that he neglects the needs of those with whom he is in his present birth connected. Though his destiny may be laid up among the stars, it is here on earth that he must train himself to be worthy of wearing the diadem of its fulfilment. When our Bodhisattva saw the starving tigress lying with her famished cubs about her, he did not turn away with the consoling thought of how much misery he would be able to relieve after the attainment of Full Enlightenment. No; with an astounding absence of attachment to his own person, and with a sublime confidence in the omnipotence of the Great Law which suffers that no jot or tittle of the result of any noble deed shall ever be lost, he flung himself into her hungry jaws, and perished. Buddhahood is to be gained by the cumulative effect of deeds of utter selflessness such as this, by the actual practice of the six great perfections of giving, morality, patient endurance, energy, meditation, and wisdom, rather than by the inert contemplation of the mere idea of any or all of them abstracted from the concrete situations, the living personal relations between one human being and another, in and through which alone they can acquire meaning and achieve realization.

Eventually, as he courses in the sixth great virtue of transcendent wisdom, the Bodhisattva comes to understand that charity must begin nearer home still, – that the 'beings' to whom he is charitable are as much mere abstractions, and therefore unreal, as 'the State', 'Wealth', 'Humanity', 'Maitrī', or any other concept; and that as the *Diamond Sūtra* repeats with such unwearied persistence, a Bodhisattva practises the great virtue of giving without entertaining the idea of a 'being'; for if he entertained such an idea he would cease to be a Bodhisattva. But considerations such as these pertain to a stage of the Path a longer way ahead than most of us are likely to reach in this birth at least, and therefore further into the subject, interesting as it is from an intellectual point of view, it would be at present unprofitable to enter.

A 'Buddhist Bible'?

THAT TRUTH IS BEYOND WORDS AND CONCEPTS, which in fact distort Reality as much as they express it, and that it is to be realized, each for himself, within the depths of a man's own consciousness, is a theme upon which most of our scriptures contain numerous and lengthy variations. The Śākyamuni Himself is represented as dwelling repeatedly on this aspect of the teaching and, indeed, from it stems much that most sharply and clearly distinguishes Buddhism from the majority of other religions – so sharply and clearly that it would perhaps be better not to class it as a religion at all.

Emphasis upon intelligent practice rather than unintelligent belief; insistence upon religion as essentially a path for active following rather than a dogma for passive acceptance; the reminder that 'the Dharma is only a raft', and that 'the finger is not the moon', together with that exhilarating exaltation of the spirit above the letter which characterizes the whole vast range of Buddhist thought and culture – all these features of the Dharma are offshoots of this one root assertion, buds of the same bush, flowers of a single tree: the assertion that adequate representation of Reality is beyond the power of thought, that scriptures are but signposts, realization the true goal. Any failure to take this into account as an aspect of the Dharma, any endeavour to minimize its importance, are mistakes fraught with incalculable danger to the entire Buddhist movement, and ones which must be corrected without any hesitation or delay.

We are prompted to make these remarks in consequence of an assertion that to compile a 'Buddhist Bible' is 'quite necessary' to the spread of Buddhism. The reasons advanced in support of this statement are, firstly, that 'It is impossible to expect a person who wants to know the essence of Buddhism to wade through the sea of literature,' and, secondly, that 'The greatest advantage which other religions have over Buddhism is that each has a gospel which everyone carries with him wherever he goes,' with its corollary that 'Buddhism suffers from not having such a handy gospel.' We shall briefly examine each of these in turn, and endeavour to find out to what extent they agree, or disagree, with the principles enunciated in the preceding paragraph.

It is true that Buddhist literature is a sea, and we freely admit that none save the most laborious scholars will ever be able to wade through the oceanic extent of all the Buddhist books in Sanskrit, Pali, Tibetan, Chinese, and Japanese. We emphatically deny, however, that it is necessary for the ordinary Buddhist even to attempt such a feat. Far from there being any need for a person who wants to know the essence of Buddhism to study whole libraries of volumes, all that such an enquirer has to do is to understand and thoroughly assimilate a single one out of the numerous chapters or even verses, into which that essence has been concentrated.

For the essence of the Dharma is not a strictly limited quantity which becomes diluted, as it were, with each successive addition to Buddhist literature (as a small amount of milk might be diluted by liberal additions of water), so that one who wishes to know it has to master an ever increasing number of books. Such a way of thinking is an example of the fantastic literalness into which a purely rational and 'practical' intelligence may sometimes be betrayed. If any comparison were needed, the essence of Buddhism might be more fittingly, though still imperfectly, represented by the flame of a lamp, which is able to kindle the flames of other lamps without the least diminution of its own brilliance.

A contributory source of the erroneous notion that a Buddhist ought to make himself acquainted with the whole enormous bulk of Buddhist sacred literature is to be found, perhaps, in the Protestant Christian belief that, since the Bible is the Word of God, the believer should acquaint himself with every single word of it, as ignorance of a single letter, even, might prejudice his chance of salvation.

It is hardly necessary to point out how utterly foreign such conceptions are to Buddhism, or to emphasize how serious is the mistake of trying to import them into it. The fundamental principles of the Dharma are few in number, and these can be explained in a very few pages well enough for most practical purposes. The multiplicity of Buddhist scriptures is due to the desire of generations of writers to elaborate these principles to the furthest possible extent, to pursue their implications into the remotest fields of thought and, above all else, to their eagerness to adapt them to the understanding and temperament of inconceivably numerous classes of sentient beings – an eagerness which has its origin in Compassion, in the aspiration that every birth-and-death-doomed creature should one day open the Door of the Immortal.

Turning now to the second reason advanced in support of the assertion that it is 'quite necessary' to compile a 'Buddhist Bible', we can at once observe how closely it is connected with the first, so that, if one be disproved, the other can be disproved also. We do not, however, altogether deny the truth of the contention that 'The greatest advantage which other religions have over Buddhism is that each has a gospel which everyone can carry with him wherever he goes.' But in what sense is the word 'advantage' to be understood? No doubt the writer means to say that Christianity and Islam (the only two religions to which his remarks are strictly applicable) have been able to spread more widely than Buddhism chiefly because each possessed a sacred book of comparatively limited dimensions.

In the first place, it may be objected that even if it were possible to accelerate the spread of Buddhism by the compilation of a 'Buddhist Bible', such an advantage would be gained only at the cost of Buddhism ceasing to be Buddhism, since the whole complex of ideas from which the Christian conception of the Bible originates are, as we have already pointed out, absolutely repugnant to the principles of the Dharma. Something might indeed be spread by such means, but it would not in truth be Buddhism, however prominently it might display that sacred name.

In the second place, it may be pointed out that, far from not possessing 'a gospel which everyone carries with him wherever he goes', Buddhism in fact possesses a number of such gospels, if by the term 'gospel' we understand simply an abridged but unambiguous statement of the most important teachings of the Buddha, and not a single divinely inspired, and hence sacred, infallible text. Any advantage in this respect would, therefore, appear to lie with Buddhism rather than with any of the other religions.

Moreover, it might be urged that Christianity and Islam were able to spread so widely in recent centuries, not because of the advantage conferred on them by the gospel they bore in their left hand, so much as by that bestowed by the sword which they wielded so ruthlessly with their right. And if a negative instance were needed to complete the induction, there is that of Hinduism which though it possessed a divinely revealed and infallible sacred book – the four Vedas – was hardly able to spread beyond the borders of India.

We therefore conclude that the compilation of a 'Buddhist Bible' would by implication involve the rejection of some of the most important and characteristic features of the Dharma, that such a compilation is in fact unnecessary, as Buddhism already possesses a large number of works embodying the essence of the Dharma, so that no one really has to wade through a sea of literature in order to know it; and that, far from it being true that 'Buddhism suffers from not having such a handy gospel,' the Dharma continues to spread as it spread so wonderfully in the past, from country to country and from heart to heart, not by the one broad highway of any gross and materialistic method, but along numerous subtle and spiritual by-paths of its own tracing.

This is not to deny that fresh compilations from the Teachings be from time to time needed, even as they were needed in the past, to meet the changed requirements of the age, and the special aptitudes and inclinations of modern men and women. All that we are concerned to deny is that any such compilation could ever be regarded as the sole vehicle of Buddhism, much less still be exalted into that supreme position of infallible authority which the word 'bible' connotes. For this would be to pollute the pure and living waters of the Dharma with the dead carcass of dogmatism, thus betraying the Master whose name we profess to bear, the Doctrine which we have vowed to follow, and the holy Order which we aspire to serve.

Autumn Thoughts

BEAUTIFUL INDEED IS THE INDIAN AUTUMN, but most beautiful of all here in the foothills of the Himalaya. The rains are over and gone, and one has no longer to huddle day after day within doors listening to the thunder of them on the roof, or watching the jagged lightning as it glares from end to end of the sky swollen with black clouds. Doors and windows are all open now, open to the warm golden sunlight glistening on the grass, on the long green hair of the earth, as she emerges from the rains as a naiad with dripping locks from the river. The human heart also expands and opens, unfolding petals of brotherhood and love. People meeting in the cool of the evening eagerly renew the acquaintanceship of last year, and friends who have not met for a season, turning aside from the highways and the heat at noon, lose themselves in the coolness of the forest and once more wander hand in hand through the deep silence of innumerable trees.

Autumn comes with flower-enwoven locks. Zinnias, marigolds, and dahlias grow wild in every hedge, and in gardens the late white roses glimmer at evening like the ghosts of the red. The flowers of the gingerlilies hang incredibly sweet from their fat juicy stems, like clouds of white and golden butterflies, so that the passer-by half expects them to take flight at his wondering approach. On the underside of millions of leaves butterflies burst the chrysalis and hover in blue and golden splendour from flower to flower down a thousand garden paths, even as the winged psyche which they symbolize bursts asunder the age-old bonds of selfhood and joyously dances from multicoloured experience to experience down all the paths of life.

Gazing into the valley one can see the fields of Autumn rice descending in a succession of narrow, sinuous terraces of emerald green to where, more than a thousand feet below, the river winds like a silver ribbon through the purple shadows of the hills, seeming to make a cyclopean stairway for the coming and going of the soft white clouds. The hills on the other side of the valley are even steeper and more rugged than our own, some of them affording no foothold for the narrowest and most precariously perched strip of cultivation. The very trees seem to find difficulty in clinging on. Here and there the sharp white fingers of the rain have left long red scars on the cheek of the earth, and in several places the landslips have loosened huge masses of soil and rock. But a catastrophe such as this, though great enough to sweep away a whole hamlet, leaves upon the faces of these ancient hills a mark hardly more perceptible than that which the fleeces of the cloudlets make in passing by. They stand as they have stood from of old, heaving their giant shoulders above the clouds, and gathering up their ridges into two dark blue peaks that stand sentinel at either end of the range-long sweep of the huge saddle-back, above and beyond which the jagged white masses of the Himalaya with blinding brilliance seem almost to float in the midst of the sky, the great peak of Kanchenjunga towering aloft into the heavens like the Thought of Enlightenment rising in the mind of the Bodhisattva.

And the sky, the blue Autumn sky! The tongue of Sarasvatī herself could hardly describe the unimaginable depth and delicacy of its colour, or even hint at the purity and transparency of the atmosphere it overarches, the invigorating freshness, the tranquillizing coolness, of the morning and evening dew. Without a cloud from noon to noon – for the clouds have fallen asleep deep in the bosom of the hills – the sky spreads like a canopy of blue silk above the earth, a celestial fabric which ranges from dawn to dusk through every heavenly chromatic variation from the palest turquoise to the deepest sapphire. Here one can realize what an eye for metaphor had the Tibetan sage who said 'The Mind is like the sky.' Mind in its natural state of purity, before the clouds of ignorance and desire have risen from the naked horizon of egoity to obscure its brilliance, is like the cloudless Autumn sky. Like the Indian Autumn sky, that is to say, as it bares its bosom to the children of the Himalaya, not like the heavens of less favoured climes, where the sky is choked with dead clouds, and wherefrom the red light glares down fiercely upon the cowering earth. Not like those northern latitudes where clouds hang low and swollen and black, as though they could no longer contain their fury of rain and hail, and were about to burst forth and discharge them violently upon the stricken fields. Such Autumn skies as these were a more fitting symbol of the state of our phenomenal minds, choked as they are with illusions as a river with weeds, than of Mind transcendental, wherefrom even the faintest vestige of ideation has utterly vanished, even as the foam-crest falls back and dies into the sea, or as the last trace of white vapour melts, in these sun-drenched Autumn days, imperceptibly into the blue abyss of noon.

In an environment and atmosphere such as this, amidst the simplicity and sublimity, the almost savage grandeur, of the foothills of the Himalaya, the waves of unquiet thought subside, our minds become by degrees clearer and more tranquil, emotions are purified from all taint of attachment, the physical body is freshened and invigorated. And as the rich Autumn days pass by as though to strains of deep and solemn music, as week after week the snow-peaks of the Himalaya stand in silence before us like an embodied ideal, we feel as though we were being enfolded ever closer and closer to the bosom of Nature, and that resting there we could feel through all the multiplicity of her veils and vestures the beating of her mighty mother-heart.

GLIMPSES OF BUDDHIST NEPAL

GLIMPSES OF BUDDHIST NEPAL

WHETHER OR NOT IT BE TRUE that there are as many kinds of Buddhism as there are Buddhists, it is undoubtedly a fact that those who have derived the greater part of their knowledge of the Dharma from the writings of Western and Western-trained scholars understand it and feel it quite differently from those who have been more deeply, because less consciously, influenced by it through the medium of a traditional environment – who from their earliest years have breathed Buddhism as they breathed the air. This fact was impressed upon me in a particularly forcible manner during my recent visit to Nepal. We have grown accustomed to treating Buddhism as though it was a mere historical phenomenon like the building of the Great Wall of China, or the Wars of the Roses. We read that it was 'founded' by Gautama the Buddha, and compute the vicissitudes of its history by the five-and-twenty centuries which have elapsed since then. The Buddha's statement that He had but rediscovered the Ancient Path traversed by the Buddhas of old evokes from us no deep or genuine response. Even if we do not dismiss the previous Buddhas as so many mythological multiplications of one original historical figure, they nevertheless appear remote and unreal to us, and fail to exercise any deep or decisive influence upon the course of our spiritual life. But this is by no means the case in Nepal. As one goes about visiting the holy places, as one sees the spot where Kāśyapa Buddha preached His First Sermon, or learns that the great Swayambhu Chaitya is four thousand years old, or beholds with a thrill of emotion the cairn which marks the place where our Bodhisattva gave His body to feed the starving tigress, one becomes conscious of a bewilderingly immense extension of the 'dark backward and abysm of time'; the petty perspectives of recorded history are enlarged an hundred- and a thousand-fold; the curtains of millennia are as it were suddenly raised and reveal to the dizzied spectator depth upon bottomless depth of time past, sphere within sphere of cosmic forebeing conglobed about the inmost dimensionless point of the infinitely long ago. Nor are those awful vistas empty and void of life, but on the contrary crowded with gigantic and majestic forms. Far back as the exhausted mind can reach rise the figures of Buddhas and the disciples of Buddhas, of Bodhisattvas and the disciples of Bodhisattvas, and the farther back it travels the more thick and numerous do those figures become until at last the mind wanders hopelessly lost among the very infinity of them, even as the eye among the numberlessness of the stars at night.

Emerging from that plunge into the abyss of the past one begins to realize how vast is the stage on which is enacted the drama of Buddhism, a drama without beginning and without end, the acts whereof are innumerable aeons, the theme Enlightenment, the actors all sentient beings. One begins to realize that the Dharma is not a product of the sixth century BCE, but that, on the contrary, it comes down producing countless Buddhas and Bodhisattvas from the beginningless past, and goes on producing countless Buddhas and Bodhisattvas into the infinite future. Faintly dawns a vague understanding of the reason for which the Dharma bears the epithet *sanātana*, eternal, which, as the commentaries inform us, simply means *paurāṇika*, ancient or old. Perhaps, though, it would be more accurate to describe this experience of the eternal nature of the Law in emotional rather than in intellectual terms, as a mysteriously vague but nonetheless potent feeling rather than as a more or less clearly defined conception. For a feeling it undeniably is, this feeling of the eternity of the Dharma which one gets in Nepal, a feeling conveyed by so many of its incredibly ancient temples and chaityas, so many of its legends, so many of its religious rites and social observances. Nowhere else in the world, perhaps, can one feel so strongly, so deep in one's being, the reality of those great world-cycles whereof all traditions speak. Nowhere else can one feel so intensely, or with so keen a thrill of faith and devotion, the over-shadowing vastness of the presence of those great World Teachers whereof all Āryan records retain some memory, however dim and obscured. Nowhere else can one feel so vividly the inexhaustible strength and vitality, the sheer stupendous duration, of that great Law which overarches the ages, to whose eternity the coming and going of Buddhas is as the coming and going of Spring to the bosom of the earth. And as one lives, as Nepal lives, in this feeling of incredible ancient-ness, this sense of eternity which bathes the whole land like an atmosphere; as one's narrow historical perspective is enlarged into a magnificent panorama of cosmic periodicity; and as one learns to see the Dharma as a universal Truth and Law without limit in space and without period in time, – then one begins to feel how firm and unshakeable is the basis of things, how fixed and unalterable, how adamantine. With this feeling of the om-nipresence and omnipotence of the Dharma, of what Sir Edwin Arnold called 'belief in the indestructibility of final good', arises a feeling of security, a sense of rest and repose. The troubles which disturb the world outside dwindle to their true dimen-sions. Our terrified anticipation of the possible destruction of the world by atomic energy appears childish and absurd. For the world, like the millions of creatures that inhabit it, has been born and died thousands of times in the past, and must die and be reborn thousands of times more in the future. Birthless and deathless only the Truth endures.

*   *   *

There are other aspects of Nepalese life which are, in their own way, no less suggestive of that beginningless prehistoric past into which recede and disappear the few score centuries of the world's recorded history. If the larger monuments of Nepal convey such an impression by their sheer antiquity, the smaller ones convey it more indirectly but no less effectively by their staggering multiplicity, and by their unbelievable richness of ornamentation. When one sees a geological formation miles high, and composed of innumerable strata; and when one reflects that hundreds, perhaps thousands, of years went into the making of a single inch-thick layer of rock, then one realizes how incalculably old the whole formation is, how ancient its mountains, how hoary with age its hills. And when one looks down through the clear blue waters which girdle some Pacific isle, sees the huge masses of delicately tinted pink and red coral branching up like great trees from the bottom, and considers how long it takes how many tiny creatures to add a single inch to their growth, then once again one's brain has to grapple with the thought of almost infinite duration, of millions of years of silent labour beneath the surface of the sea. Similar is the impression produced by the amazing multiplicity of the chaityas, viharas, and temples of Nepal; by the thousands of tiny shrines which cluster at the corners of the streets; by the tens of thousands of carved wooden windows, doors, and posts, by the millions of images, the miles of painted banners, the acres of hammered work in brass and copper, silver and gold. One feels that the production of such tremendous artistic wealth must have kept a whole nation busy for hundreds, if not for thousands of years. So enormous, indeed, is the number of objects which have been accumulated, and so unmistakably does each bear the stamp of the same fantastic beauty, that the spectator even feels like attributing their production to the inexhaustible fecundity of some great natural force rather than to the labour of mere human hands. This impression is heightened by the minuteness, delicacy, and intricacy of much of the work. Leaving aside examples of craftsmanship in metal, ivory, and wood – materials which easily lend themselves to fine workmanship – and taking instead an example such as the Maha Bodhi temple at Patan, one finds that every single square inch of its exterior surface has been carved with a tiny image of the Buddha, on a scale so minute that it at once reminded me of a passage in one of the sūtras which says that a Buddha together with His company of Bodhisattvas is contained in every grain of dust – a symbolical way of expressing the truth that every phenomenon in the universe contains indestructibly the potentiality of *bodhi*.

It would not be just, however, seriously to attribute to nature what has in fact been created – unbelievable as the magnitude of the achievement might make it appear – out of the deep musings of human hearts by the loving skill of human hands. To the Newar artists and craftsmen of Nepal, especially to those of the Kathmandu valley, belongs almost exclusively the credit for producing all these lovely things, just as to the Gurkhas belongs almost exclusively the credit for safeguarding for so many years the freedom and independence of the country so effectively that the indigenous arts and crafts, together with all else pertaining to a way of life founded on traditional values, could flourish and bloom undisturbed in the fertile soil of peace. If the Newars, the predominantly Buddhist inhabitants of the pleasant and fertile Kathmandu valley, are more cultured, of more refined tastes, of keener aesthetic sensibilities, more skilled in arts and crafts, cleverer at administration, trade, and commerce, than are the predominantly Hindu tribes inhabiting the surrounding hills who are loosely grouped together under the name of Gurkhas, then it may with equal justice be said that the Gurkhas are not less strikingly distinguished from the Newars by their superior physical strength and moral courage, by their greater straightforwardness, honesty, and loyalty. In a word the difference between the Newar and the Gurkha is the difference between a predominantly passive and feminine, and a predominantly active and masculine, temperament. This fact was impressed upon me more than once during the two weeks which I spent in Nepal. At the various expositions of the sacred relics of the Lord Buddha's chief disciples, Śāriputra and Maudgalyāyana, which were held in Kathmandu, Patan, and Bhatgao, I could not help noticing that it was the Newars who invariably formed the body of the worshippers, who came with devotional songs on their lips and flower-garlands in their hands. The khaki-clad Gurkha troops, with their rifles slung over their shoulders, remained standing in the background, handling the swarms of excited people with good-humoured efficiency, considerably less demonstrative than the Newars, perhaps, but in their own way no less keenly participating in and enjoying the sacred function. On such occasions as these I could not help reflecting that the history of how many countries showed that the intermingling of peoples of seemingly antagonistic, but in reality complementary, temperaments, was one of the most important factors contributing to the development of rich and harmonious national cultures. Perhaps it would not be too fanciful to see in the Newar and Gurkha types an ethnic adumbration of that great dualism which runs through the whole of nature, of those mysteriously separate and mysteriously united principles which in the Vajrayāna Buddhism of Nepal are known as *Prajñā-Upāya*, and symbolized by a male and female figure locked in inseparable embrace. Just as the

Bodhicitta, the Thought of Enlightenment, is produced by the interpenetration of the passive and active elements of personality, so may it be possible to produce, by the gradual fusion and amalgamation of the two principal ethnic stocks of Nepal, not only a united people but a common national culture that will combine strength with refinement, emotional plasticity with intellectual precision, truth with beauty, love with life.

* * *

While in Nepal I was frequently told, usually by Hindu friends, that one of the happiest features of life in that hitherto secluded country was the perfect amity in which Buddhists and Hindus lived. The words 'Buddhist' and 'Hindu' are in fact unknown there, except among a small English-educated minority, the terms in general use being *Bauddha-margi* (follower of the Buddha's path) and *Shiva-margi* (follower of Shiva's path) respectively. Now it must be observed that, contrary to the generally accepted modern humanistic mode of thought, tolerance is in itself not necessarily a good thing, nor always an unmixed blessing. While it is undoubtedly a good thing to exercise tolerance in the sense of allowing others to entertain beliefs and follow practices different from those which we entertain and follow ourselves, it is definitely not a good thing to pretend that such differences do not exist. The vague statement that all religions are equally true comes perilously near the more precise one that all religions are equally false. This is not so much tolerance, as indifference. There can be true tolerance only when genuine differences of view-point are not only admitted to exist, but accepted as inseparable from the limitations of human understanding and the inalienable right (and duty) of every individual to work out his own salvation with diligence. The adoption of such a position, however, does not mean that we should refrain from opposing beliefs and practices which we sincerely think are at variance with what is true and good, or from endeavouring to reform social customs and observances which, in the name of religion, are in fact perpetrating cruelty and injustice. The Buddha Himself did not hesitate to condemn in the strongest possible terms erroneous doctrines such as *ātmavāda*, vicious social institutions such as the caste-system, and inhuman customs such as that of animal sacrifice. It is regrettable that the Buddhists of Nepal, partly from a mistaken understanding of what constitutes tolerance, have allowed themselves to adopt from Hinduism institutions and observances so utterly un-Buddhistic as the caste-system and animal sacrifice. Although it is true that this betrayal of Buddhism by the Buddhists themselves was to a certain extent due to political pressure brought to bear on them by the forces of brahminical orthodoxy, it is nevertheless equally true that had it not been for the mistaken tolerance of the Buddhists during their period of political ascendancy those forces would never have been in the position to exert such an influence later on. By all means let the Buddhists and Hindus of Nepal continue to live, as they have lived for centuries past, in peace and harmony. Such examples of mutual tolerance in the religious world are not so plentiful that it can afford to dispense with even a single one of them. But let the Buddhists beware of purchasing that peace and harmony at the price of being untrue to the teachings of their own religion. Let them rather convince their Hindu brethren of the evil and injustice of the system of hereditary caste, of the cruelty and uselessness of the ritual killing of living creatures, and live with them in the peace that comes when men realize that they are all brothers, and the harmony that arises when they look with compassion on the sufferings of all sentient beings.

*   *   *

With the question of the reform of Buddhism in Nepal arises, inseparably linked to it, the question of its revival there. More than once, as I sat listening to the numerous and lengthy speeches which were delivered at the various functions held in honour of the sacred relics, I heard pronouncements which might have led one to suppose that a revival of Buddhism was, if not actually sweeping like fire from one end of Nepal to the other, at least about to do so at any minute. While sympathizing with the hopes of those who, in the boundlessness of their optimism, fondly imagine that the revival which we all agree to be desirable is actually taking place, one is nevertheless compelled, in the interests of truthfulness, to dissent from such a superficial analysis of the situation, and to say plainly that such a revival is neither taking place at present, nor very likely to take place in the near future. Of course, if one thinks of Buddhist revival in terms of large public meetings presided over by members of the government, of processions with scores of motor-cars and dozens of lorries, of highly emotional speeches, or putting more and more people into yellow robes – and a section of people certainly do seem to think of it in this way – then perhaps it can be said, with more or less accuracy, that some such revival has taken place. But it is not in terms such as these that we think of the revival of Buddhism in Nepal or any other country. The temptation so to think is indeed great, particularly in the midst of the excitement and enthusiasm of a big religious celebration, but it must be resisted, and an effort made to review the situation calmly and dispassionately. The significance which is attached to the expression 'the revival of Buddhism' depends largely upon the significance which is attached to the word 'Buddhism' itself. If one is understood superficially, the other cannot but be understood superficially also. When we allude to the revival of Buddhism in Nepal we are thinking not of the introduction of the social observances of a particular sect, but of the revival of that spirit of universal wisdom and boundless compassion which it is the object of the doctrines and practices of all sects to attain, and in which the essence of Buddhism above all else consists. Now a revival in this sense cannot truthfully be said to be taking place. The most that can be claimed is that conditions are today much more favourable to such an occurrence than, by all accounts, they were a few years ago. But whether the opportunities for the revival of Buddhism which undoubtedly do exist in Nepal today are being laid hold of in the right way, or whether such seeds as have already been sown in the religious field are likely to germinate and bring forth flowers and fruit, is a matter for independent consideration and judgement. These are only glimpses of Nepal, not a complete perspective, and at present it is not possible to do more than make a few observations and offer one or two suggestions.

To begin with, it must be observed that the Buddhism of Nepal is a branch of the great banyan tree of Mahāyāna Buddhism which even now overshadows the greater part of Asia. Most Nepalese Buddhists are followers of the Vajrayāna, that is to say, the Adamantine Path or Vehicle (an unsatisfactory translation!), and it is therefore from the doctrines and practices peculiar to the Tantric form of Buddhism – a form no less authentic than any other – that the Buddhism of Nepal derives its distinctive features and individual character. It should therefore be hardly necessary to point out that the first step towards any revival of Buddhism in Nepal is to strengthen the forms in which the doctrine already exists there. Even admitting, for the sake of argument, that the meaning of many of those forms has in the course of time been forgotten or misunderstood, the people are at least familiar with them, since they have been woven into the texture of their lives from childhood, and it would be far easier to remind them of the forgotten significance of forms with which they were already familiar, than to teach them doctrines which they did not understand through the medium of forms with which they had no previous acquaintance. I was therefore sorry to see that some of the people engaged, as they thought, in the revival of Buddhism, could find no better way of effecting it than by ridiculing and condemning the beliefs and customs of the overwhelming majority of Nepalese Buddhists, and by endeavouring to popularize among them the social practices of certain other Buddhist countries in the mistaken conviction that they were thereby introducing 'Pure Buddhism' into Nepal! An attitude of mind such as this betrays a serious incapacity to distinguish between what is essential in Buddhism and what adventitious, between what pertains to the outer form and what to the inner spirit. One is compelled to assume that persons so obsessed by externals have no personal experience of the more spiritual side of Buddhist life at all. What little genuine Buddhist spirituality I encountered in Nepal (and I am confident that had I been able to stay longer I should have encountered much more) I found not among the foreign-ordained revivalists, but among those upon whom they looked down with so much disdain, among the followers of traditional Nepalese Buddhism. How well I remember the evening service in one of the incredibly ancient and unbelievably beautiful viharas of Patan! Aloft on the altar at the far end of the chamber stood a silver image of the thousand-armed Avalokiteśvara. Innumerable lamps were burning, and shed a soft lustre on the dark crimson pillars and yellow frescoed walls. A long row of yellow-robed figures, one of men, the other of women, sat on the right and left side respectively of the nave of the shrine. They chanted with half-closed eyes, their hands assuming various mudrās, and the sound of their chanting was sweet as the music of birds in the trees of Sukhāvati. At a signal from their leader, a stout, dignified old man who sat on a throne nearest the altar, holding the vajra in his left hand and the bell in his right, the deep-throated Tibetan trumpets would roar, and the drums beat, until the whole place trembled and shook with spiritual vibrations. Then again the brisk sweet chant would rise up like a wave, and the row of shaven-headed old women sitting opposite me would sway themselves gently to and fro, eyes closed, their wrinkled faces shining in the soft golden light of the lamps, absorbed within themselves and oblivious to the sights and sounds of the outer world....

As we stole from the shrine, my friend and I, and crept down the uneven stairs into the darkened streets, and heard the sound of the chanting dying away behind us into the distance, I could not help feeling that it was in an atmosphere and environment such as this, profoundly peaceful yet full of hidden life and secret activity, that there might be engendered a spiritual impulse dynamic enough to bring about a revival of Buddhism in Nepal. Deep, deep down into its roots does the juice of life sometimes retreat, so deep that, seeing how dead and dry are the leaves and branches which it once vivified, one might think that it had left them for ever. But when it rises with the return of Spring, and once more courses vigorously through a thousand tiny veins, so that the erst bare branches are again covered with leaves and flowers, then one knows that the life had not gone, but was simply waiting, that it was not dead, but only fast asleep. With the help of such a simile as this might be set forth the present condition of Vajrayāna Buddhism in Nepal, and an indication given of the richness of the potentialities which are undoubtedly lying hidden beneath the centuries-old accumulation of what its critics describe as 'meaningless' rituals and 'superstitious' doctrines. As well ridicule the barrenness of a tree in Winter as the seeming degeneracy of a religious tradition which has for the time being withdrawn into its sources. Such a tree is more likely to burst into bloom when the time comes, than is a branch brought from some foreign clime and simply intruded by main force into the native soil. It is unfortunate that some members of the Sthaviravāda Sangha, so recently introduced into Nepal, and still with difficulty maintaining a precarious hold on the fringes of Nepalese religious life, should be able to discern the withered leaves of Vajrayāna Buddhism clearly enough, yet should be quite blind to the vital forces lying coiled up within its roots. It may be true that the Vajrācāryas, or hereditary gurus of the Vajrayāna order, in all but a very few cases no longer possess the spiritual authority which alone can entitle them to occupy in society the exalted position which is traditionally their prerogative. But should this point be unduly insisted upon, or should it be emphasized in an invidious manner, then it would not be surprising if the Vajrācāryas and their disciples were to remind their critics that the leaves on the Sthaviravādin tree were not a whit less dry and withered than those on their own, and that their antagonists were apparently no nearer to Arahantship than they themselves were to Bodhisattvahood. But such mutual recriminations would serve no useful purpose whatsoever, and it is a pity that the Sthaviravādins should have so unwisely laid themselves open to so obvious a rejoinder. The few dozen Hīnayāna bhikṣus, śrāmaṇeras, and anāgārikas of Nepal have as yet no provision whatsoever for study, whether of secular or religious subjects. Few are able to preach even elementary Buddhism, and it appears that none of them is versed in the practice of meditation well enough to be able to instruct others. With a state of affairs such as this obtaining, it would surely be better for all alike to devote their energies to the task of self-improvement, rather than to waste them in unhelpful criticisms which only serve to accentuate old differences and to create new ones, thus delaying still further the making of a united effort towards the revival of Buddhism in Nepal in the highest sense in which the expression can be used.

*   *   *

Swayambhu! The name rolls echoingly along the corridors of the mind and, reverberating in the inmost chambers of memory, rouses associations that have slept for a thousand years....

Swayambhu, holy of holies of Nepal, sacred hill, how often did I lie awake in the early morning, while it was still dark with a cold blue darkness, tinged here and there with white mist, before the birds had begun to raise their tremulous winter notes, listening to the bands of worshippers as they swung with full-throated chorus up to the top of the hill, where the great white dome and gleaming golden spire of your chaitya tower gigantically into the heavens! How sweetly and clearly the music of those songs drifted across the hillside, through the waning moonlight, into the darkness and silence of the vihara where I lay. Like echoes from another life they seemed to come, growing louder and more insistent as the day dawned, until at last, as though in response to their summons, I rose from my bed once again, and found most of the other inhabitants of the vihara already astir.

Shantiniketan it was called, the Abode of Peace, and whether because of the proximity of the sacred precincts of Swayambhu, half way up the slopes of whose hill it was situated, in the midst of thick groves of trees wherein chattered and played innumerable bands of red-rumped monkeys, or whether because of the aura of the people who lived there, I do not know. But certainly the vihara was a most peaceful place, so peaceful that it was with a feeling of relief and thankfulness that I returned to it each evening after an interesting, but long and tiring, day of public meetings, lectures, entertainments, and other functions in the city, and found the two youngest boys waiting at the head of the stairs in eager anticipation of my arrival, while their elder brothers busied themselves lighting the fire and preparing tea in the kitchen downstairs. It was like returning home. Relaxing my limbs on the carpeted and cushioned floor of the long, low upper room, with the four calm bright faces in a semi-circle round me, and surrendering myself to the waves of peace which came softly flowing in upon me from all sides, I felt that I had found one place at least on earth which had escaped the 'contagion of the world's slow stain', and wherein the distant restless tumult of modern life had as yet been able to raise no disturbing echo. As I sat sipping the glass of tea they had brought me the father of the four boys would come in (wrapped in a quilt, for he had only recently recovered from an attack of fever), his sons rising respectfully to their feet as he entered. He was tall for a Newar, well built, and in his youth must have been more than ordinarily good-looking, even as his sons all were now. But the most striking feature of his appearance, and the one by which an observer was immediately attracted, was the smile which ever hovered like a sunbeam about his lips as he sat and talked, and the calm effulgence with which his face continually glowed, as though a light had been lit within. He never raised his voice, but his words had a peculiar force and intensity; and although he spoke so rapidly that at times I had difficulty in following what he said, he never spoke excitedly, but always seemed profoundly at peace, conveying in this respect an

impression similar to that of the broad and impetuously rushing, yet deep and fundamentally tranquil, current of some
mighty river. It transpired that his wife had died many years
before, and that not long afterwards he had resigned a lucrative
government appointment in order to devote himself exclusively
to the study of religion and the practice of yoga. Sometimes
living in temples, sometimes roaming about naked, and sometimes retiring into remote jungles and dwelling in inaccessible
caves where (I heard later from one who had spent a few days
with him in such a place) supernatural beings of frightful appearance visited him in such numbers that no other person
dared to remain there with him, step by step he had advanced
upon the hard and dangerous path of spiritual training, gradually acquiring in the course of his practice not only calm and
illumination of mind but also various supernormal powers
which, he told me one evening, had arisen spontaneously and
become, as I could see for myself from the number of people
who came to him for advice and instruction each day, the means
of attracting numerous disciples and devotees.

Many were the hours which I spent with him in the chill
winter evenings, listening to the placid torrent of his conversa-
tion, ringed by the kneeling figures of his quartet of quiet and
attentive sons. Occasionally he would call upon one of them to
explain something that he had learned, but the youths were
invariably tongue-tied in their father's presence, nor did their
organs of speech loosen until he had good-humouredly quitted
the room with a parting instruction to let me hear what they
knew. Sanskrit grammar and literature, together with Buddhist
philosophy, were the only subjects which they had been permitted to study, and in these they appeared fairly proficient, being
in fact able to converse a little in Sanskrit. Of history and
geography, as well as several other subjects deemed indispens-

able by the modern educational system, they were completely innocent. It was astonishing to see how easily ignorance of the most elementary facts of modern life could co-exist with a more than superficial knowledge of the abstruser side of ancient Buddhist thought. These white-garmented young hermits had never heard of London, and were unacquainted with the locations of England and Japan; but they had studied such works as the *Prajñā-pāramitā* and the *Guhyasamāja*, and at least one of them could explain without difficulty the metaphysical chapter of the *Bodhicaryāvatāra*. As I became more intimately acquainted with them, and began to feel the charm of their spontaneous and affectionate natures, I could not help thinking how far-sighted was the decision in consequence of which they had been able to dwell for so many years with the profound and simple things of the Dharma, rather than amidst the corruptness and complexity of modern urbanized and industrialized living. Their seeming ignorance was only the space which had been allowed for the tree of wisdom to grow in. The astonishment would in fact have been more appropriately felt by such as they than by such as we – astonishment that 'educated' people could so unthinkingly lose sight of the eternal in the midst of the transitory, the essential in the midst of the unessential. Only one of them, the youngest, showed any symptom of curiosity about what went on in the world outside the boundaries appointed by their father. For the most part, they appeared happy in the studies and meditations prescribed for them, and content, even eager, to prepare themselves towards the ripening of the time when they would be, like their father, Vajrācāryas not only by birth but by attainment, thus fulfilling his aspiration that they should become, one day, exemplars and preachers of the Dharma to thousands of their fellow-countrymen.

Perhaps the time that I was able to spend in that peaceful vihara on the slopes of the sacred Swayambhu hill were, from the spiritual point of view, the most valuable part of a visit so rich in impressions that many a year must pass before they are all thoroughly assimilated. Certain it is that within the four walls of that unpretentious building, in the midst of that unique family, I came in contact with traditional Nepalese religious life in one of the purest and most authentic forms in which it is possible for it to exist today, and was vouchsafed what I believe to have been my brightest glimpse, even as it will remain my most luminous memory, of Buddhist Nepal.

THE PATH OF THE INNER LIFE

THE PATH OF THE INNER LIFE

RELIGION IS NOT A MATTER FOR BLIND BELIEF or intellectual assent, but for living faith and energetic practice. It consists not in the acceptance of any creed or dogma but in the achievement of an experience, or rather in the achievement of a number of experiences. These experiences link up into a series. This continuous series of experiences forms a Path or Way. When we consider it with regard to its direction it appears as an inward-going as opposed to an outward-going Way, as a Path of the Inner rather than of the Outer Life. Since it is a matter of immediate personal experience within the heart-depths of the individual devotee, and since such experience is by its very nature incommunicable, it is spoken of as an Esoteric as opposed to an Exoteric Path, as a Doctrine of the Heart rather than as a Doctrine of the Eye. When we realize that those experiences are not simply aggregated round any unchanging ego-entity or permanent core of separate selfhood, but that they are, on the contrary, processes of progressive self-impoverishment, self-annihilation, the Path appears as a Way of Emptiness; but, since the 'seeming void' is in reality 'full', it also appears as a Way of Compassion. Finally, when we regard it as a Path which runs not only between but also above all mind-made dualities, it is seen as a Middle Way.

When speaking of the Path of the Inner Life we automatically contra-distinguish it from the Path of the Outer Life. The distinction consists not so much in a difference of position as in a difference of direction. That is to say, it is to be understood not statically but dynamically. The Path of the Inner Life is also known as the *Nirvṛtti Mārga* or inward-circling path and that of the Outer Life as the *Pravṛtti Mārga* or outward-circling path.

That which 'circles' either inwards or outwards is the mind. The natural tendency of the mind is to spread itself out fan-wise, as it were, over the five objects of the senses. This outward-circling or fan-wise spreading movement of the average human mind is naturally accompanied by a corresponding disturbance of the psychic harmony of the subject and a diminution of the sum total of his psychic energy. Just as the brilliance of a beam of light diminishes as it is spread out over a wider and wider area, so the power of the mind decreases as it is scattered over a larger and larger number of objects. The more concentrated the mind becomes, the more powerful it grows, and the more deeply it is able to penetrate into the fathomless abyss of Truth. The mind which is engrossed in the pleasures of the five senses is uncon-centrated and therefore impotent. It is unable to see things as they really are. The Buddha and His enlightened disciples of all ages and climes proclaim as though with one voice that *prajñā* or transcendental wisdom arises only in the concentrated mind, and that the mind becomes concentrated only when it is puri-fied of all taint of earthly desires.

The first step along the Path of the Inner Life, without which no other step can be taken, is to become 'indifferent to objects of perception'. Such indifference is never the result of satiety, but is, on the contrary, the slowly-ripening fruit of constant perseverance in stern renunciation. 'Do not believe that lust can ever be killed out if gratified or satiated, for this is an abomina-tion inspired by Māra', warns *The Voice of the Silence*.[1] The early stages of the career of a spiritual aspirant are a period of unceas-ing struggle between the lower and higher impulses of his nature. On the outcome of this struggle depends the success or failure of his vocation. If he is able to resist the solicitations of the objects of perception and turn his senses as it were inside out, like the five fingers of a glove, thus reversing their direction, they will merge into a single inner sense, and with this subtle inner sense he will be able to perceive spiritual realities. Mystical religion has therefore ever stressed, as indispensable preliminaries to any attempt to know the Truth that will make us free, the killing out of all desire for sense-pleasures and the withdrawal of the scattered forces of the mind into a single unified focus of attention. Only by becoming deaf and blind to the outward illusion can we develop that subtle 'inner touch' that will enable us to intuit the Truth that sounds and shines within.

But this purely spiritual perception of spiritual realities by the inner spiritual sense differs from that of our other states of consciousness, inasmuch as it does not take place within the framework of the subject–object relation. The chasm which ordinarily yawns between the experient subject and the object of his experience becomes more and more narrow until finally it disappears and he knows the Truth by becoming one with it. Therefore it is written: 'Thou canst not travel on the Path before thou hast become that Path itself.' In the vigorous words of the Buddha, we have to 'make the path become'. This path-becoming is therefore also a self-becoming, a process of self-development, self-transformation, self-realization. The Goal of the Path, the Ultimate Experience in which the whole long series of experiences eventually culminates, is the state designated as Nirvāṇa.

Since the Path of the Inner Life consists essentially in a series of experiences, and since all experiences are by their very nature ineffable, it is also an Esoteric as opposed to an Exoteric Path. Nothing in the religious life is truly esoteric save spiritual experience. The most private ritual, the abstrusest philosophical doctrine, the most jealously guarded scripture, the most secret society or organization, are all exoteric. They belong to the domain of 'Head-learning' rather than to the domain of 'Soul-wisdom' and, as *The Voice of the Silence* emphatically admonishes us, it is above all things necessary to learn to separate the one from the other, to learn to discriminate between 'The Doctrine of the Eye' and 'The Doctrine of the Heart'.

Many, unfortunately, think that the secret teaching consists of some piece of information about the evolution of the universe or the constitution of man which has not been communicated to the world at large, and that it is necessary to acquire this information from certain mysterious personages supposed to be hiding themselves in inaccessible corners of the earth. Such 'secret teachings' or, for the matter of that, whole libraries of secret scriptures and orders of secret teachers may indeed exist, but they all belong to the Exoteric Path, to the domain of Head-learning, and are of little value in the spiritual life. Indeed, they are often in the highest degree harmful to it, for those who believe that they have learned the 'esoteric doctrine' and become 'initiates' generally grow so proud of their fancied superiority to the rest of mankind that for them progress along the true Esoteric Path is barred for a long time to come. That is why *The Voice of the Silence* is 'Dedicated to the Few'. The *Hṛdaya Dharma* or Heart-Doctrine which was transmitted by the Lord Buddha to His immediate disciples, and which was handed on by them to their disciples and their disciples' disciples, even down to the present day, does not consist of any formulated doctrine, much less still any written scripture, but was simply His own ineffable experience of Nirvāṇa. The true Esoteric Path, the true Secret Teaching, the true Doctrine of the Heart, the true Master, is not to be found in any book, or, indeed, anywhere at all in the outside world, but in the heart-depths of the spiritual experience of the individual devotee.

Although the Path of the Inner Life, the Esoteric Path, consists of a series of experiences eventually culminating in the Supreme Experience designated Nirvāṇa, these experiences are not 'acquisitions' of the subject in the sense that material things and even learning are acquisitions. The one root-illusion which prevents us from seeing things as they really are, and which it is the primary business of spiritual practice to remove, is the belief in ourselves as separate, perduring individual selves or ego-entities. Inseparably linked with this belief is the feeling of possession, the desire for acquisition. The concepts of 'I' and 'mine' are simply the two sides of a single coin. As, therefore, the aspirant progresses along the Path of the Inner Life or, better still, as he more and more becomes that Path, the false sense of separative selfhood, the feeling of possession, and the greed for acquisition are simultaneously attenuated and eventually disappear altogether. The further, therefore, the aspirant progresses along the Path, or the more truly he becomes it, the harder it is for him to dichotomize his experience into a subject and an object and to speak of the latter as though it was a possession or acquisition of the former. In the Supreme Experience of Nirvāṇa such a claim would have become a complete impossibility. The Buddha therefore declared that those who laid claim to any spiritual attainment as though they had made it their personal property thereby only betrayed the hollowness of their pretensions.

The decisive test of whether any experience is truly spiritual or not consists in ascertaining whether it is possible to speak of it as 'my' experience or not. If it is possible truthfully to speak of it in this way it is simply an addition to the mental or emotional furniture of the ego and as such is merely mundane. This is the meaning of the choice which the aspirant is called upon to make between the 'Open Path', the Path of the pseudo-

Arahant, and the 'Secret Path', the Path of the Bodhisattva. The Arahant is popularly supposed to be one who is indifferent to the miseries of sentient beings and therefore does not remain on earth to help them but disappears into the private bliss of a purely individual Nirvāṇa; whereas the Bodhisattva is supposed to be one whose heart is so profoundly moved by the woes of the world that he decides to renounce the 'sweet but selfish rest' of Nirvāṇa and to devote himself to the alleviation of human misery even to the end of time. The choice which the aspirant has to make between these two Paths constitutes his severest test and final initiation.

Although the popular doctrine represents both the Open Path and the Secret Path as genuine alternatives, the Way to Nirvāṇa is in fact only one. The Path of pseudo-Arahantship, of individual liberation, in fact represents the temptation to think of the Supreme Experience as something which can be possessed privately by the individual subject. The renunciation of the thought that Nirvāṇa is something to be attained is the last condition precedent for the 'attainment' of Nirvāṇa. Where there is the feeling of possession, of 'my-ness', there is also the sense of separative selfhood, of 'I-ness', and so long as this sense of separative selfhood persists, liberation is impossible, for liberation is fundamentally nothing but liberation from this same root-illusion of separative selfhood. Neither Arahantship nor Bodhisattvahood, which are simply the same realization in predominantly intellectual and predominantly emotional perspectives, can be attained without the complete renunciation of the ideas of 'I' and 'mine'.

The Path of the Inner Life is spoken of as a Way of Emptiness because it consists in the progressive attenuation of the ego-sense, and the gradual intensification of the realization that everything is devoid of separative selfhood, that all is intrinsic-

ally pure and void. This void is not, however, a zero or nothingness. Buddhists express this truth by saying that the Void is itself
void. Just as the 'seeming full' is void, so also the 'seeming void'
is full. This fullness or rather overflowingness of the seeming
void is what we call Compassion. Since Compassion is not an
inert principle or a static somewhat but a purely transcendental
activity, it is frequently personified as Amitābha Buddha,
Avalokiteśvara, Kwan Yin, etc. In the magnificent but still inadequate words of *The Voice of the Silence*,

> Compassion is no attribute. It is the Law of LAWS – eternal
> Harmony, Alaya's SELF; a shoreless universal essence, the
> light of everlasting right, and fitness of all things, the law of
> Love eternal.

The more attenuated the ego-sense becomes, the more abundantly will selfless activities be manifested, for the Way of
Emptiness is also the Way of Compassion, and to become one
therefore means to become the other also. Emptiness and Compassion, Wisdom and Love, are the static and dynamic aspects,
respectively, of the one Supreme State of Nirvāṇa. The Arahant
ideal stresses the former, the Bodhisattva ideal the latter; but the
goal is the same for both, and the eradication of the ego-sense
is indispensably necessary in either path. Self-enlightenment
and compassionate activity for the sake of all sentient beings are
mutually exclusive alternatives only on the level of the dichoto-
mizing intellect. In reality they are the intension and extension,
the depth and the breadth, of a single realization which is at once
both emptiness and compassion.

The Arahant ideal is unattainable by him who imagines that
he has an individual self which is in bondage and which must
be liberated: the self is the bondage. The Bodhisattva ideal is

unattainable by him who imagines that there are separate individual beings for him to save.

Buddha said: 'Subhūti, all the Bodhisattva-Heroes should discipline their thoughts as follows: all living creatures ... are caused by Me to attain Unbounded Liberation, Nirvāṇa. Yet when vast, uncountable, immeasurable numbers of beings have thus been liberated, verily no being has been liberated. Why is this, Subhūti? It is because no Bodhisattva who is a real Bodhisattva cherishes the idea of an ego-entity, a personality, a being, or a separated individuality.'[2]

Emptiness and Activity, *Prajñā* and *Karuṇā*, Wisdom and Compassion, are in reality not two but one, which is ineffable Nirvāṇa, and the paths which lead thereto, the Path of the Arahant, and the Path of the Bodhisattva, are also one, which is the One Way (*Ekayāna*), the Way of the Buddha (*Buddha-yāna*).

Finally, since the Path of the Inner Life avoids such extremes as those of self-indulgence and self-torture, Nihilism and Eternalism, self-reliance and other-reliance, individualism and altruism, together with the mutually exclusive deformations of the 'Arahant' and 'Bodhisattva' ideals, it is spoken of as the *Majjhima Patipada* or Middle Way. It should not, however, be supposed that as such it is simply a compromise between two antagonistic positions or an effort to solve antinomies on the same level of experience at which they arise. The Middle Way lies not so much between extremes as above them. It is not the lowest common denominator of two contradictory terms but the Higher Third wherein both find perfect mutual solution. The numberless antinomies which arise on the ordinary levels of human experience can be resolved only by attaining to a relatively higher level of experience. Intellectual problems are finally solved only by spiritual realization. To follow the Middle Path means to cultivate the practice of solving the conflicts of life and the contradictions of experience by rising above the level at which they are possible. The Middle Way is therefore essentially a Way of Spiritual Experience, and as such coincides with the Path of the Inner Life. Since all such conflicts and contradictions are products of the ego-sense, and can be solved only by rising above it, it also coincides with the Way of Emptiness, and therefore with the Way of Compassion too.

When we see that the Path of the Inner Life, the truly Esoteric Path, the Way of Emptiness and the Way of Compassion, and the Middle Way, are all aspects of the One Way, the Way taught by the Buddha, we begin to glimpse the profound truth of the saying that 'The Path is one for all, the means to reach the goal must vary with the Pilgrims.'

Religion as Revelation
and as Discovery

The study of the science of Comparative Religion, inaugurated in Asia by the Buddha (*Dīgha Nikāya, Brahmajāla Sutta*) and in Europe by Roger Bacon (*Opus Majus*), is one of the most fascinating subjects to which the mind of man can possibly devote itself. The spectacle of the millennia-long struggle of humanity towards the Truth cannot fail to arouse the deepest and most poignant emotions in the breast of him who contemplates it with genuine interest and sympathy. For the history of Religion is, in fact, the history of man; not, indeed, of the peripheral and accidental man, but of the central and essential man; not of his physical body and material environment, but of that profoundest and most pregnant part of him which we may call his mind or heart (Indian *citta*, Chinese *hsin*). It is not the history of the memorable deeds he has done, of the great empires he has founded, of the immense wealth he has wrung from the bosom of nature, but of the character which he has formed, of the degree of inner illumination which he has attained, or of what, in a word, he has become.

The totem and fetish of the savage, to say nothing of the religious doctrines and philosophical systems of his civilized descendants, awaken in us vague feelings of sympathy which is almost reminiscence. For we are all bound on the same pilgrimage, have passed through the same stages of development, and therefore hold in the present moment of our consciousness the accumulated inheritance of all that man has ever thought and felt and done. We have sacrificed our children to Moloch, we have severed the sacred mistletoe with a sickle of gold, we have danced in drunken frenzy on the moonlit hills of Thrace; and we, too, perhaps, have listened enraptured to the Sermon on the Mount, or heard some Buddha, Bodhisattva, or Arahant unfolding before us the mysteries of the good Law. The *saṁskāras* or active impressions created by those experiences still live within us and vibrate whenever the simulacrum of the object which originally imprinted them appears.

The study of the Science of Comparative Religion is therefore in truth the study of the evolution of our own consciousness. Herein lies the secret of its tremendous fascination. Moreover, it enables us, when properly studied, to see the various grades and species of religious experience not as isolated or unconnected events in man's mental life, but as the intimately interrelated component parts of a great pyramid of consciousness the apex whereof is the Consummation of Incomparable Enlightenment (*Anuttara Samyak Sambodhi*).

But the researches and investigations which a host of anthropologists, archaeologists, philologists, and historians have been making for more than a century have placed before the student of Comparative Religion such a bewilderingly rich variety of material in such astounding qualities that he is now in grave danger of being unable to see the wood for the trees. It has thus become imperatively necessary to divide religions into types and classes in order to transform the chaos of mere unrelated facts into the cosmos of an exact science. We are familiar with such divisions as natural and revealed; true and false; natural, anthropological, and psychological; of finite mind, infinite mind, and absolute mind; theistic, atheistic, pantheistic, and so on. Others more elaborate and strictly scientific have also been suggested. But that division of religions which we are about to consider is not only perhaps more fundamental than any of these but moreover of vital importance in the dharmic or normative life.

The problem of whether Religion is essentially a revelation of truth *to* man or a discovery of truth *by* man is in fact the intellectual formulation of a spiritual difficulty which each one of us experiences in the course of his or her quest for Reality. The most obvious and natural grouping of the various religions and sects of the world is, therefore, into those for whom Religion consists in revelation, and those for whom it consists of discovery, of the Truth. This division is not simply theoretical, since each of these definitions of Religion has exercised a profoundly modifying influence upon the entire body of the beliefs and practices of the religions which were, whether consciously or unconsciously, dominated by it. Perhaps it was with the thought of some such division in his mind that Stanislas Schayer wrote of Buddhism as 'the most profound and most fundamental antithesis to Christianity'.[3] Nor is this division wholly new. Far-Eastern Buddhists have long been familiar with the classification of religions into those depending on 'self-power', in Japanese *jiriki*, and those depending on 'other-power', or *tariki*. And in India religious aspirants are sometimes spoken of as displaying the characteristics of the young monkey, which clings fast to the hair of its mother's belly, and of the kitten, which is simply carried about helpless in her mouth.

Religion-as-Revelation holds that the existence of Religion in the world, and therefore the possibility of the attainment of Salvation or Emancipation by man, is ultimately dependent on the Object, the Other, and that the initiative in the matter belongs wholly to It or Him. It conceives the spiritual life not as the progressive actualization of a perfection potentially present in man but as the acceptance of something which he would never have been able to acquire by means of his own unaided

efforts. Consequently, it tends to stress the weakness and sinful-
ness of human nature and to emphasize the necessity of extra-
terrestrial intervention in the affairs of humanity. It is therefore
only natural that Reality should be conceived as personal, and
that the founders of the various religions and sects should be
regarded as prophets or messengers (*nabi, rasul, messiah*) sent
from, or as full or partial incarnations (*avatāra*) of, Him. The
written record of the message, teaching, or life of each such
founder is invariably regarded as the word of God Himself, and
to doubt, question, or criticize it is considered not only to
preclude all possibility of salvation but even to run the risk of
eternal damnation. Religion-as-Revelation therefore places the
strongest possible emphasis on faith in God, faith in His
prophet, messenger or incarnation, faith in His infallible Word,
faith in His Church, faith in His priest. Unfortunately, the beliefs
of the various founders, scriptures, and churches which are
included in this group of religions often disagree not only
among themselves but also with those which are included in the
other group. Hideous fanaticism and ferocious persecution thus
ensue. Since each such religion regards its own particular revelation as the supreme and incontrovertible source of Truth the
possibility of an appeal to reason and experience is automatically precluded. Obviously God would not wittingly contradict
Himself. One revelation must therefore be true, and the remainder false, that is to say, not revelations at all but simply human
fictions and inventions. Moreover, Religion-as-Revelation's
house is divided not only against itself but against many other
houses as well – against Science, for instance, which has succeeded in demonstrating the fallibility of many an infallible
scripture. Is it, then, a matter for wonder that Religion-as-
Revelation is fast losing its hold upon the hearts and minds of
reflective men and women throughout the world?

Religion-as-Discovery, on the other hand, holds that Religion is essentially a manifestation of the human spirit, that man is able to discover the Way to Truth himself by means of his own unaided human efforts, that the attainment of liberating knowledge depends upon the subject or self, and that the initiative in the matter rests ultimately within the abysm of one's own volition. It would envisage the dharmic or normative life not as the engraftment of some exotic blossom on to the barren stock of humanity but as the flowering forth of its native perfection from the seed within. Consequently, it is inclined rather to inspire man by appealing to his innate strength and goodness than to discourage him by dwelling upon his mistakes and failures. Instead of imagining an arbitrary divine intervention to be the most important event in history it asserts the supremacy of natural law and maintains that the aspiration towards emancipation must, like every other process, proceed in accordance with an eternal and universal order (*sanātana dharma*). It is therefore hardly surprising that Religion-as-Discovery conceives Reality as a suprapersonal principle of knowledge or state of consciousness or that it regards the religious founder simply as one who, after himself realizing that principle or state, teaches humanity the way thereto. The records of his life and teachings are only a map describing the Way, a raft to cross the stream, or a finger pointing to the moon. They demand not blind faith but clear-sighted understanding, they appeal not to some infallible authority but to reason and experience. Religion-as-Discovery is therefore not only tolerant of all other religious beliefs and practices, howsoever divergent from its own, but is able to join hands with earnest seekers after truth in every sphere of human activity. It sees Science not as an enemy but as a friend and fellow worker.

The last two paragraphs have presented the two principal conceptions of Religion in what may be described as their 'chemically pure' state. But if we are to proceed in accordance with the spirit of the Science of Comparative Religion we shall not leave them in a position of uncomfortable antithesis but will try, instead, to discover the psychological basis of their divergence. This will not only enable us to understand their mutual relation but also to determine their respective positions in the hierarchy of consciousness.

Understanding is impossible without sympathy. Let us therefore project ourselves, as it were, into the mind of one who feels the necessity of revelation and try to understand his condition from within rather than from without. The two elements which play the chief roles in such a mind are an intense aspiration towards Reality and an overwhelming sense of its inability to attain thereto. A feeling of continual frustration therefore naturally ensues and in time becomes so intense that the subject is willing to adopt any available means of bringing to a speedy end the terrible stress and tension by which he is tormented. It is therefore with a sense of tremendous relief that he casts the whole responsibility for his salvation upon the shoulders of the Other. He receives with joy and gratitude the gospel of salvation by simple faith and goes out in an ecstasy of adoration towards whoever proclaims that it is sufficient to trust in Him.

Upon extricating ourselves from the antinomy of such a consciousness we are naturally prompted to ask why it should have been unable to attain to Reality by means of its own unaided efforts. In order to answer this question we shall have to consider in what cultural and religious environment this antinomic consciousness most commonly arises.

The matter is not difficult to determine. The three extant Semitic religions, Judaism, Christianity, and Islam, are clearly all dominated by the conception of Religion-as-Revelation. All believe in a self-revealing God, all possess an infallible sacred book, and all believe, albeit in different ways, in someone supposed to be sent to man from God. Let us also consider in what cultural and religious environment the opposite type of consciousness most commonly arises. Buddhism and Taoism are perhaps the only religions which consistently adhere, in their oldest and most authoritative scriptures, to the conception of Religion-as-Discovery. Hinduism as a whole wavers uncertainly between the two conceptions. The Yogadarśana, which is affiliated to Buddhism, inclines for instance toward one, while the two Mīmāṁsās, which are weighed down by the burden of Vedic authority, and various devotional schools, which are theistic and incarnationist, incline toward the other.

Having thus determined which religions and sects conceive Religion as revelation, and which regard it as discovery, we are in a position to enquire whether there is present in the various systems belonging to each group any common factor which predisposes them to view Religion in the two ways described. Such a factor there indeed is. It is the presence in Buddhism of a graded path of *śīla, samādhi,* and *prajñā* – a clear and comprehensive Way leading progressively from the lowest point of mundane to the loftiest pinnacle of supramundane consciousness and its absence in Judaism, Christianity, and Islam, that is the principal cause of the difference between their respective conceptions of Religion. It is a startling but nevertheless completely verifiable fact that neither in the Old Testament of the Christians, nor yet in the Muslim Koran, is there anything even remotely approaching the scheme of systematic self-culture comprised in the Middle Way or Āryan Eightfold Path of Buddhism. Christ has truly said that 'The Kingdom of Heaven is within you'; but the Christian Scriptures contain only a few scattered and unconnected hints on how to realize it. The same may be said of Judaism and Islam.

It is, of course, true that each of these three great faiths produced a large number of spiritually gifted men and women who not only regarded Religion as discovery but even progressed along the Path themselves and described many of its stages for the benefit of their friends and followers. Such were the Cabbalists among the Jews, the Mystics among the Christians, and the Sufis among the Muslims. But these persons were not only regarded with the gravest suspicion, and even violently persecuted, by their more orthodox co-religionists, but are regarded by modern students of Comparative Religion as being subject to strong influences of Indian origin. Thus A.C. Bouquet, an Anglican clergyman, writes '... the pseudo-Dionysius [universally regarded as the fountain-head of medieval Christian mysticism] is only superficially Christian, and has a quite different religion as its real basis.... Mysticism of the non-Christian type is perfectly at home in the religious life of Indians. Hence those parallels to the Christian mystics of the Middle Ages which have been found in Hindu and Buddhist literature and to which attention has been drawn, are not in the least surprising, and do not mean that the Christian mystics in question have an affinity with the Hindus by virtue of their Christianity, but purely in consequence of their having steeped themselves in a particular apocryphal writing, which is based upon the writings of the Levantine pagan mystic, Proclus.'[4] Dean Inge, the celebrated modern representative of Christian Neoplatonism, has been branded, like Shankara in India, as 'a disguised Buddhist'. Sufism developed largely in consequence of the spiritualizing influence exercised by Buddhism and Vedanta on primitive Islam. Even Taoism is not wholly free from the suspicion of Buddhist influence. We moreover observe that with the growth of mysticism, whether in its Jewish, Christian, or Muslim forms, there is a corresponding development of the characteristics associated with the conception of Religion as essentially a process of discovery and realization. The great mystics are consequently disinclined to stress the infallibility of any scripture, declaring instead that the light can shine forth only from within; they display a rare tolerance and breadth of vision which the fanaticism and narrow-mindedness surrounding them serve to make more conspicuous; they proclaim with one voice that Religion is a Path to be followed, a Realization to be won, not a ritual to be performed or a creed to be believed.

Conversely, when certain Buddhist sects, such as that founded by Nichiren, degenerated into Religion-as-Revelation, and began to regard the Buddha as a self-revealing deity, the *Saddharma-puṇḍarīka Sūtra* as His infallible revelation to mankind, and Nichiren himself as His inspired messenger, and, in a word, began to exhibit all the characteristics of the conception of Religion as essentially revelation, they naturally adopted an intolerant and hostile attitude towards all other sects. Needless to say, they laid more stress on faith in the Deity, the Scripture, and the Prophet than in the cultivation of the threefold Path of *śīla, samādhi,* and *prajñā.* Scarcely better is the attitude of certain pseudo-Theravādins who maintain that it is impossible to tread the Path or attain Nibbāna in the present age, and that one should, therefore, simply fold his hands in resignation and await the advent of Metteya Buddha. The careful student of Comparative Religion will be able to discover numerous examples of this highly significant correlation of the presence or absence of a progressive Path with the conception of Religion-as-Discovery and Religion-as-Revelation respectively.

We are now able to see that these two principal conceptions of Religion are not merely antithetical, but that one is comprehended by the other. The Middle Way or Āryan Eightfold Path exists everywhere, for suffering exists everywhere; but it is not always perceived. Those who do not perceive it, together with those who, having perceived a little of it and trodden it to that extent, naturally feel the need of revelation and tend to think of Religion as something that satisfies that need. Religion-as-Revelation is not opposed to, or unconnected with, Religion-as-Discovery, but is simply the product of a psychological difficulty which arises when one is either unable or unwilling to tread the Path to its end. Religion-as-Revelation is included in Religion-as-Discovery just as a stage of the Path is included in the whole Path, and as our partial and fragmentary mundane consciousness is comprehended in the supra-mundane universal consciousness of Supreme Buddhahood.

The 'Problem' of Ahiṁsā

THE THEORETICAL CONSIDERATION OF SPIRITUAL TRUTHS, without the actual practice of them in daily life, generally results in intellectual confusion. What was crystal clear to the heart of the devotee becomes an insoluble problem in the eyes of the mere philosopher. Such has been the case with the great principle of *ahiṁsā*. It is torn out of the living context of actual practice and, after being applied to all sorts of imaginary situations and impossible exigencies of conduct, it is treated as a problem which calls for merely intellectual solution. One is asked whether he would use violence to protect the chastity of his mother or his sister, or whether he would feel himself justified in taking the life of one man in order to preserve the lives of a hundred men. It is furthermore pointed out that, since life is able to exist at all only by crowding the weaker forms of life out of existence, a completely non-violent life is a contradiction in terms, and the doctrine of *ahiṁsā* consequently an impossible ideal, a mere counsel of perfection, which cannot be realized at all in this violent world, and the logical consequence of which is, or would be if life followed logic, simply suicide. Having thus thoroughly confused his own mind and the minds of those who were foolish enough to listen to him, the armchair philosopher triumphantly concludes that it is quite useless even to try to practise *ahiṁsā* and that one had better let the world go on in the same bad old way that it did before one was born and will go on, presumably, after one is dead.

The first thing that we shall have to do before we can clean up this intellectual mess is to decide in what *hiṁsā* and *ahiṁsā* really consist. The Buddha has made it clear that the criterion by which the ethical status of an action is to be determined is the purity or impurity of the state of mind by which it was inspired. The mind is said to be pure when it is free from desire (*lobha*), hatred (*dosa*), and ignorance (*moha*), and impure when it is not free from these three defiling tendencies. An action is ethical or unethical not because it conforms to or does not conform to a predetermined scheme of dos and don'ts but because it is rooted in states of mind which make for liberation or which make for bondage. *Hiṁsā* and *ahiṁsā* are therefore primarily states of consciousness in which hatred (*dosa*) and love (*adosa*) respectively predominate. We shall see later on, however, that although they are essentially attitudes of mind rather than specific actions they nevertheless tend to express themselves outwardly in the field of life and action in a determinate manner.

Since *ahiṁsā* is fundamentally a condition of heart or a state of consciousness, the practice of *ahiṁsā* must consist primarily in the cultivation of that condition or state. It does not consist in the observance of any number, however large, of rules, nor in the observance of any system of precautions, however elaborate, against even the accidental taking of life. What we may designate as the legalistic view of *ahiṁsā* is an attempt to solve the 'problem' of non-violent action purely on the intellectual plane; it does not succeed in rising to the level of spiritual perception. It tends to make the practice of *ahiṁsā* a mechanical observance rather than a flaming passion. *In the sphere of ethics to try to determine what one should do before one has found out what to think and how to feel is a case of 'putting the cart before the horse'.*

The particular defiling tendency of mind to which violence (*hiṁsā*) is affiliated is, as we have already seen, hatred (*dosa*). The practice of *ahiṁsā* therefore consists in the eradication of hatred (*dosa*) and the cultivation of love (*adosa*). But since hatred (*dosa*) is, like desire (*lobha*), in turn affiliated to ignorance (*moha*), the practice of *ahimsā* consists, in the last analysis, in the eradication of ignorance (*moha*) and the cultivation of wisdom (*prajñā, bodhi*). *Ahimsā* resolves itself into love, and love in turn resolves itself into knowledge, for action depends upon feeling, and feeling in turn depends upon understanding. *Ahimsā* is 'the outward and visible sign of an inward and spiritual grace', the external expression of an internal realization. We should try to find out what that understanding, grace, or realization is, for without it the practice of *ahimsā* is impossible.

To begin with, it is necessary to understand correctly in what ignorance essentially consists, for knowledge is in its negative aspect nothing but the absence or privation of ignorance. The Buddha has repeatedly affirmed that the one root-illusion which proliferates into all the miseries and misconceptions to which our mortal flesh is heir, which lies at the back of every greedy, cruel, or deluded thought or word or deed, is the tightly-clung-to belief that we are individual selves or separate ego-entities which are divided by an impassable gulf of difference from all other similarly constituted selves or ego-entities whatsoever. To this view, in its most refined no less than in its grossest formulations, the Buddha gave the name of *ātmavāda* or philosophical Egotism. He made it perfectly plain that wheresoever lurked even the subtlest sense of separative selfhood there lurked also incipient the germs of greed, cruelty, and delusion, and therefore of birth, disease, old age, death, and every other form of suffering too. Because men think and feel themselves to be little hard cores of separative selfhood, with interests and ambitions which differ from, or at times even directly clash with, the interests and ambitions of all the other millions of similarly constituted 'selves', they naturally behave and act as such, and their behaviour and actions are naturally either centrifugal movements of attraction to the 'pleasant' which we call desire (*lobha*) or centripetal movements of repulsion from the 'painful' which we call hatred (*dosa*). It is not difficult for a child, even, to understand that *ātmavāda*, egotism, or, in plain Anglo-Saxon, selfishness, in one or another of its innumerable forms, is the root cause of all the wickedness, and therefore of all of the misery, which has ever been or which ever will be in this or in any other world. When selfish interests and ambitions are thwarted they turn into hatreds which are violent in proportion to the strength of the frustrated desire; and violence is but another name for *hiṁsā*. Only by thoroughly uprooting the minutest fibres no less than the thickest and toughest stems of the ego-sense shall we be able to check the wild growth of hatred and arrest the exuberance of the swelling buds from which runs down the world-intoxicating wine of violence. It is for this reason that the Buddha stressed the indispensable necessity of the eradication of the ego-sense in the spiritual life and laid down the doctrine of *anātman* or *Śūnyatā* as the ultimate philosophical foundation of His religion.

Since ignorance (*moha*) consists primarily in the belief that one is, has, or contains some kind of permanent and peculiar element called 'soul' or 'self', wisdom (*prajñā, bodhi*) on the contrary consists in the knowledge that one's own and all other 'personalities' or 'things' whatsoever are altogether empty of any such entity, and that one's mind is a stream of psychic events even as one's body is a stream of physical events. For the foolishness of the conception of a static being is thus substituted the wisdom of the realization of a dynamic Becoming. Into the genesis of the illusion of permanence it is not our intention now to enquire, but irrefragably true and certain it is that until this most pernicious of all illusions is destroyed root and branch the full and perfect practice of *ahiṁsā* is impossible. To try to practise non-violence while clinging desperately to the conception of a permanent individual soul or self is like trying to row a boat which is still fastened by its hawser to the shore. The cultivation of what we may term the sense of universal emptiness is the one fundamental spiritual practice which all others must subserve. Any practice which heightens one's ego-sense, howsoever holy in popular estimation it may be, is unspiritual, and any practice which attenuates it, howsoever mean and despicable outwardly it may seem, is spiritual in the truest and best sense of the term. Growth in holiness is essentially growth in emptiness. But it should not be supposed that emptiness is equivalent to the absolute death of a blank annihilation or nothingness. Certain ignorant and malicious critics of Buddhism have indeed persistently tried to misrepresent it as such, despite the unanimous emphatic declaration to the contrary of all schools of Buddhist thought. Emptiness or egolessness is equivalent to blank annihilation only to those for whom the conception of a life of egolessness is consequently unthinkable. But those who do not thus fondly cling to the illusion of selfhood, who have learned, in the terse words of *The Voice of the Silence*, to see 'the voidness of the seeming full', to understand the egolessness of all this ego-seeming existence, are able to see also 'the fullness of the seeming void', to realize that emptiness instead of being a mere negation pulsates with spiritual life – with that pure and perfect life which, although appearing to our dualistic consciousness as the Life of Compassion, thinks not 'I am compassionate.'

It would be a mistake, however, to think of emptiness and egoless compassionate activity as two distinct principles, or even as two merely accidentally related states. They are to each other as the obverse and reverse sides of a single coin, or indeed even more intimately related than that – so intimately in fact that in the end it becomes impossible to speak of a relation at all, since to do so implies that they are in a sense external to each other, like the distinguishable although inseparable sides or angles of a triangle, whereas in truth emptiness is active and activity is empty. The realization of one is therefore necessarily the realization of the other also. If one wishes to achieve the condition of compassionate activity, which is the positive expression of the rather negative and contentless term *ahiṁsā*, one must first of all attain to the state of emptiness or egolessness. The 'problem' of *ahiṁsā*, or in fact any other difficulty experienced in applying ethical principles to concrete situations in daily life and exigencies of personal conduct, arises only when it is sought to attach non-violent actions in a purely external manner to an egotistic and therefore fundamentally violent consciousness. The ego can act only egotistically. It is impossible for it to act egolessly. Only emptiness can act egolessly and compassionately and therefore non-violently also. The ego-dominated intellect is totally unable to penetrate the mystery of egoless activity. Its artificial attempts to create patterns of non-violent behaviour without first of all removing the root-cause of violence are foredoomed to failure from the very beginning. The realization of emptiness is the only way to achieve egoless, compassionate, and non-violent activity for the benefit of all sentient beings.

When the ego-sense is removed compassionate activities, or in negative terminology non-violent behaviour, will stream forth spontaneously from the purified inner consciousness, just as, when the boulders which blocked its passage are removed, the mighty mountain torrent rushes downward to the plain below. Problems of conduct will no more arise. 'His mind becomes peaceful, so also his speech and deeds,' sings the *Dhamma-pada*. Conduct will automatically be non-violent when the consciousness behind it is non-egotistic. Situations which seemed to present insoluble theoretical difficulties will be entered into and solved spontaneously by enlightened practice in a manner baffling the comprehension of the ego-ridden intellect. But, although these subtler activities of emptiness in its more refined phases and more delicate shades of manifestation may elude the clumsy grasp of the dualistic understanding, the general pattern of its activity is nevertheless distinctly recognizable.

The Buddha has stated clearly and categorically that one who has realized the perfection of emptiness, and therefore also the plenitude of compassionate activity, is incapable of transgressing the fundamental rules of ethical behaviour, although for such a one obedience to the moral law indeed consists not so much in the acceptance of a code imposed from without as, on the contrary, an expression of a realization flowering spontaneously from within. Although the Arahant is 'beyond good and evil' he nevertheless manifests in the field of life and action in a determinate manner as an ethical, not as an unethical, being. Buddhism thus bangs the door in the face of antinomianism and sternly rejects the pseudo-liberation which claims that one who has transcended all such relative terms as good and evil is capable of acting indifferently in a manner which is moral or in a manner which is immoral according to the canons of conventional ethics. The purely transcendental activity of ineffable emptiness manifests in the world of relativity as compassion, or rather is apprehended by it as such, and *ahiṁsā* or non-violence is simply the negative expression of a particular phase of that manifestation. As we have already said, *ahiṁsā* resolves itself into compassion, and compassion in turn resolves itself into egolessness, for action depends upon feeling, and feeling in turn depends upon understanding. Only the empty and egoless, the loving and compassionate, can practise *ahiṁsā*. For them only the 'problem' of *ahiṁsā* does not arise. They alone are blest. They alone are the true Bodhisattvas, the true Śrāvakas.

THE NATURE OF BUDDHIST TOLERANCE

FACETIOUS QUESTION HAS BEEN MADE whether words reveal or conceal thought more. The kernel of truth contained in this dry old husk of a jest becomes apparent when we review the efforts made by the translators of Eastern philosophical and religious texts to render terms like *karma, nirvaṇā, citta,* and *dharma* each by a single equivalent word in a modern language: one may be pardoned for feeling that all their labours have succeeded in obscuring, rather than in clarifying and illuminating, the idea which the original author sought to express.

Dense as the obscurity of verbally equivalent translations is, however, it is as nothing compared with the obscurity which ensues when Eastern philosophical and religious systems are described in terms to which there is not the remotest analogy, even, in the languages through which their ideas were originally conveyed. It is often said, for example, that Buddhism is a tolerant religion, and that during the two-and-a-half millennia of its historical existence it has exhibited tolerance unparalleled by any other creed; but neither in Pali nor in Sanskrit does any word exist of which 'tolerance' might serve as even the most approximate translation. Swami Vivekananda has said that the word 'intolerance' is not found in the Sanskrit lexicons because this socio-religious phenomenon was not found in India. Apart from the fact that the statement is historically false (for intolerance undoubtedly *did* exist in ancient India, and both Buddhists and Jains had from time to time to endure its force and fury), it might with equal truth be argued that since the word 'tolerance' is not found in Indian dictionaries, the phenomenon of tolerance is unknown in Indian life. Crudities of this sort will have to be avoided if we wish to solve the problem of how it was possible for Buddhism to exhibit the characteristic of tolerance to such a marked extent when, apparently, it had no clear conception of this particular virtue, and never sought deliberately to infuse it among its votaries. But first of all we shall have to form a clear idea of the meaning of the word upon which our whole discussion revolves.

Etymologically, the transitive verb 'to tolerate' is derived from a Latin root meaning 'to bear', and it is of interest to note that this root is akin to the Greek *tlenai*, to bear or to endure, whence is derived Atlas, the name of the giant who in Hellenic mythology supports on his shoulders the pillars of the sky. As used in English literature the word means, in addition to the primary sense which it has inherited from its Latin ancestor, firstly 'To suffer to be, or to be done, without prohibition or hindrance; to allow or permit negatively, by not preventing; as, to *tolerate* doubtful practices,' and secondly 'To bear the existence of thorough indifference or lack of interest; to put up with.'[5] Though originally applied to disagreeable things, persons, or occurrences, it was not long before the application of the word was enlarged so as to include opinions and ideas on all subjects, but particularly those connected with religious doctrines and beliefs.

The nouns 'toleration' and 'tolerance' are the results of this extension. By toleration is meant the 'Act or practice of tolerating; specif., the policy, usually governmental policy, of permitting the existence of all (or given) religious opinions and modes of worship contrary to, or different from, those of the established church or belief; recognition of the right of private judgement, esp. as to religious matters,' while by tolerance is meant 'The act, practice, or habit of tolerating; the quality of being tolerant; specif., the disposition to tolerate, or allow the existence of, beliefs, practices, or habits differing from one's own; now often, freedom from bigotry; sympathetic understanding of others' beliefs, etc.'[6]

An examination of these definitions reveals that the object tolerated is in normal circumstances repugnant, or even positively painful, to the person by whom it is tolerated. When this object is a religious doctrine it becomes more painful still; for a belief which contradicts one's most cherished convictions is regarded not merely as an error of judgement, but as a personal affront, as a threat to the security of the state, and even as a menace to mankind. Our natural reaction to pain is aversion or, to pain inflicted by a living being, hatred; and hatred leads, sooner or later, to violence. That species of hatred which is excited by the existence of opinions, particularly religious opinions, contradictory to, or merely different from, our own, is known as intolerance; and the kind of violence which such hatred engenders is known as persecution. Since opinions originate not by themselves, but from human brains, intolerance is felt for, and persecution directed against, not merely the thoughts but the thinkers. In Christian Europe the burning of heretical books led quite naturally to the burning of the heretics themselves. Given the dogmatic premises of Roman Catholic theology, a philosophically-minded historian, had such a being existed in the fourth or fifth centuries CE, could probably have predicted in detail the atrocities of the wars of religion and the enormities of the Holy Inquisition a thousand years later. That the peoples of the West have become comparatively tolerant during the four or five centuries which have passed since those pious days is due to the operation of two kinds of factors, one acting externally on ecclesiastical corporations, the other internally on the hearts and minds of men.

In the first kind of factor may be included historical events such as the collapse of Papal Supremacy, the disestablishment of the Russian Orthodox Church, the strict separation between Church and State which was decreed in many countries, and, in Protestant lands, the necessity of adjusting the rival claims of a host of mutually hostile sects. All these events resulted in a drastic curtailment of the political power which had been wielded for centuries by religious bodies. They wrested the sword from the Church's bloodstained grip. Those in whose hearts the fire of fanaticism burned as fiercely as ever ceased to persecute, not because they had ceased to hate those who held convictions different from their own, but simply because the power to persecute had been taken from them. The dogmatic premises of Roman Catholicism, for instance, have not changed since the palmy days when heretics were tortured in the dungeons of gloomy castles, or with civic pomp and religious ceremony burned alive at the stake in public squares. The Church is still by no means unwilling to wound, and recent events in some of the South American republics, such as Colombia, where Protestants have been burned and drowned and tortured to death, have shown that, whenever the sword of political power is restored to her hands, she is by no means afraid to strike.

In the second kind of factor which has contributed to the comparative tolerance of the modern West may be included all those scientific discoveries which have disproved the Church's dogmas, challenged the exclusive truth of its revelation, and weakened the faith of many of its supporters. The so-called tolerance of Christian lands today is, therefore, largely due to the fact that the intolerant are rarely able to exercise political power, while those who do exercise political power seldom have so much misguided zeal for their religion that they are willing to persecute on its behalf. Such tolerance as exists is, in fact, little more than the joint product of impotence and indifference. The only kind of positive factor to be noted is the steady growth of belief in the right of private judgement in religious matters, of the freedom of individual men and women to decide for themselves what their personal attitude towards the deepest things of life will be. The third factor operates, however, on the minds of a cultivated minority, and does not exercise any direct influence on the conduct of the majority of nominally Christian folk.

The same principle of freedom of thought was not only accepted by the Buddha, but clearly enunciated and uncompromisingly upheld by him throughout the five-and-forty years of his earthly ministry. He repudiated Vedic authority and ridiculed the pretensions of the Brahmins. In the *Kālāma Sutta*, which may be described as Humanity's Charter of Religious Freedom, he advised the Kālāmas of Kesaputta, whose minds had been confused by the dogmatic assertions and exclusive claims of the sectarian teachers of that period, not to go by hearsay nor to rely on tradition, nor even on inference, nor to defer out of respect to the opinions of the professionally religious. In accordance with the severely pragmatic character of his doctrine, he urged them to submit all teachings to the test of personal experience, and to reject those which were blameworthy, which were contemned by the wise, and which would, when followed out and put into practice, conduce to loss and suffering.[7] Still clearer and more positive were the words which the Tathāgata addressed to Mahāpajāpati, his maternal aunt and foster-mother: 'Of whatsoever teachings, Gotamid, thou canst assure thyself thus: "These doctrines conduce to passions, not to dispassion: to bondage, not to detachment: to increase of (worldly) gains, not to decrease of them: to covetousness, not to

frugality: to discontent, and not content: to company, not solitude: to sluggishness, not energy: to delight in evil, not delight
in good": of such teachings thou mayest with certainty affirm,
Gotamid, "This is not the Norm [*Dharma*]. This is not the Discipline. This is not the Master's Message." But of whatsoever
teachings thou canst assure thyself (that they are the opposite
of these things that I have told you), – of such teachings thou
mayest with certainty affirm: "This is the Norm. This is the
Discipline. This is the Master's Message."[8]

By living in accordance with the Dharma, by practising its
successive stages of ethics (*śīla*) and meditation (*samādhi*), the
disciple develops an intellectual intuition (*prajñā*) of Reality by
which he is liberated from the false conception of things as
mutually exclusive ego-entities. He sees that the universe is
completely empty of all separate selfhood, and that every single
'object' in fact interpenetrates, and is interpenetrated by, every
other 'object'. It was this great vision of life which the Buddha
sought to share with humanity, which he sent forth his Arahants
to preach, and which, embodied in metal, wood, and stone,
depicted in line and colour, and described in rich and rhythmic
verse, flooded the whole Eastern world with the radiance of 'a
light that never was on sea or land'.

To bring light means to banish darkness. When knowledge
dawns, the shades of ignorance must flee away. The above
quotations from the Scriptures illustrate the fact that the
Buddha not only made absolutely clear what Dharma is but
what it is not. With unexampled insight he analysed the multitudinous philosophical views (*diṭṭhi*) and religious practices
(*vata*) of his time and, by the application of the pragmatic
principle, distinguished the true from the false, the right from
the wrong. In the *Brahmajāla Sutta*, the celebrated first discourse
of the *Dīgha Nikāya*, he classified no less than sixty-two

erroneous views, condemning them all as hindrances to the living of the holy life and the attainment of Nirvāṇa. It should never be forgotten that, for a preacher of the Dharma, to reveal truth and to dispel falsehood are the positive and negative aspects of one process, and the history of Buddhist thought bears testimony not only to the energy with which the Message of the Master was propagated but also to the vigour with which contradictory doctrines were opposed. Buddhism has never fled to that last refuge of feeble-minded philosophers, the vague but, apparently, consoling thought that all religions and philosophies are 'true', whatever this may be held to mean, and that they all lead, in the end, to the same destination, whatever and wherever it is believed to be. With the goal of the holy life shining clear before their eyes, and the path thereto stretching plain and straight from beneath their feet, the followers of the Buddha naturally sought to turn people aside from the false paths which led only to illusory goals.

But why was this never done forcibly and violently, with the rack and the stake, as in Christian Europe, or even with the help of an occasional outbreak of persecution, as in Hindu India or Confucian China? Buddhism was for centuries in possession of almost unlimited political influence, but not once did it invoke the aid of civil authority in dealing with its enemies. Even in lands where an ardently Buddhist monarch ruled over a devout people, the sole armour of a warrior of the Dharma was reason, his only weapon persuasion, as he endeavoured 'with winning words to conquer willing hearts'. For what special reason was it that the Buddhists, who believed in the truth of their religion as ardently and as uncompromisingly as any Christian bigot or Muslim fanatic, did not imitate them in the employment of political power to enforce religious conformity?

The answer to this question lies in one of the most beautiful words to be found among all the riches of Buddhist vocabulary: *karuṇā* (Compassion). We have already pointed out that violence springs always from hatred, and that persecution is simply the kind of violent behaviour which results from that form of hatred we call intolerance, which is a feeling determined not only not to bear, but even to destroy, the object of its aversion. The root of hatred, as of desire, is ignorance. This ignorance is not merely intellectual, but spiritual, and consists in the erroneous conception of 'things' and 'persons' as mysteriously ensouling an unchanging principle of individuality by which they are irreducibly differentiated from all other 'things' and 'persons' in the universe. The realization that concepts such as 'things' and 'persons' are in reality empty of such a principle, and exist instead in a state of 'unimpeded mutual solution', destroys not only egoism but also the false views and wrong emotions which are begotten by egoism. Ignorance is transformed into wisdom, and hatred, the emotional complement of ignorance, into compassion, the affective counterpart of wisdom. False views can issue in violence, since egoism has not been destroyed, and until egoism has been destroyed ignorance and hatred will continue to spring up as luxuriantly, and spread as rapidly, as weeds do when the root has not been torn out from the ground and burned. Buddhism, since it annihilates the erroneous conception of unchanging separate selfhood, stifles as it were ignorance, lust, and hatred in the womb, and permanently precludes the possibility of violence being used even for the advancement of its own tenets. The Dharma of the All-Enlightened and All-Compassionate One spares us the contradiction of spreading the gospel of love by means of the sword, and the paradox of burning alive men, women, and children who entertain religious opinions different from our own, to show how tenderly we care for the salvation of their souls.

Instead, it presents us century after century with a magnificent spectacle of compassionate activity, with an ever-changing panorama of missionary enterprise whereon, as the scene shifts from country to country, and as races, cultures, religions, and languages succeed each other with bewildering rapidity, there gleams unchangeably the steadfast light of love. That which shines forth to Western eyes, or to Eastern eyes wearing Western spectacles, as the much lauded modern virtue of tolerance, is in truth what Buddhists call *upāya*, or skilful means, the radiant offspring of the embraces of *prajñā* (wisdom) and *karuṇā* (compassion). The strength which fills the 'messenger of the Dharma' is not the restless and tumultuous energy of hatred, but the placid and serene power of Love. The light which guides him on his way is not the flickering marsh-fire of dogmatic religion, which entices to betray, but the clear and steadfast radiance of Perfect Wisdom. Compassion saves him from the extreme of fanaticism, intolerance, and persecution; wisdom delivers him from the opposite extreme of 'universalism' and indifference. Without compassion, he would sin against man; without wisdom he would sin against the Truth. Possessing both, he follows in the footsteps of the Supremely Wise and Boundlessly Compassionate One, treads the Middle Path and, practising the Perfection of Skilful Means, continues to pose to the modern world the problem of how a 'religion' which does not even possess a word whereby to translate 'tolerance' should yet be more 'tolerant' than many which do.

WHERE BUDDHISM BEGINS AND
WHY IT BEGINS THERE

THAT EXISTENCE WAS ALL OF A PIECE (whether mental or material), and that the truth about existence was therefore a whole, was, at least until fairly recent times, an article of faith more or less generally accepted among philosophers. Hence the conception of philosophy as system, as being the coherent explanation of the totality of phenomena. Hence the conception of the philosopher as system-builder, as the architect of a vast and elaborate structure wherein every fact would find its appointed place. From Plato and Aristotle to Hegel and Herbert Spencer, the ambition of philosophers has been to build ever bigger and better systems than their predecessors, just as it is the ambition of American millionaires to build bigger and better skyscrapers. Except that the philosophers have had more justification than the millionaires, for the fact-population of the philosophical world has increased enormously during the last few hundred years, and it might therefore with some plausibility be argued that extra accommodation was by this time urgently required.

If the 'truth is the whole' and if philosophy is system, it follows that both are fixed and unchanging. Their universe is what William James called a block universe. Nothing ever happens in it. Nobody goes anywhere. Nobody does anything. Everything has happened and all people have gone where they wanted to go and done what they wanted to do, once and for all. Time is somehow adventitious, progress an illusion, change unreal. Existence as a whole is what it was eternally in the past and what it will be eternally in the future. We are frozen into it as a fly into a block of ice. *Sub specie aeternitatis*, everything exists simultaneously. All the philosopher has to do is to construct an exact model of existence. Hence the appropriateness of the architectural simile. But however clear and coherent his mental blueprint may be, as soon as he commences his work of construction the philosopher is confronted by a serious difficulty. Where is he to begin? The ordinary architect is called upon to solve no such problem; whether he likes it or not he has to begin by laying the foundation. But our philosophers who build with airy concepts are not hampered by any such restraints, and may begin wherever they please, whether in the basement or the attic, down the crypt or up the steeple. Their freedom of movement is, moreover, facilitated by the fact that they are not sure in which direction 'up' and 'down' really are, since this would be to entertain preconceptions, and from all preconceptions their ideal of strict philosophical objectivity demands that they should be free; so which part of the building is the crypt and which the steeple will be known only when the structure is complete, when it stands four-square (or whatever other shape it may be) in all its rigid perfection and immobile beauty to all the winds of change that blow. In the meantime it exists clearly and coherently enough in the mind of the architect, as we have already said, and with this fact we must be content. The only difficulty is the practical one of exposition, and merely practical difficulties have never troubled philosophers overmuch.

Reduced to its simplest terms, the difficulty in which the system-building concept of philosophy finds itself inevitably involved is that of representing serially, as a succession of parts, what it conceives spatially as a simultaneity of parts; of expressing eternity in terms of time. Since reality is not like a ball of twine, with a definite beginning and end, which can be unrolled little by little until it forms one divisible and measurable line, the difficulty is, in fact, insuperable. The eternalist view of reality pictures it as a sort of sphere or globe, and how impossible it is to make a two-dimensional projection of a three-dimensional figure, all cartographers know. But books have to be written, just as maps have to be drawn, and although a philosophical work may appear to dispense with an end, it can hardly dispense with a beginning. In the absence of an objectively determinable starting-point, the system-building philosophers have therefore fallen back more or less unconsciously on their subjective preferences and made do with those.

Descartes began with *cogito, ergo sum*, though for no better reason than that the scholastics who had preceded him began with revelation. Spinoza took as his point of departure axioms which he thought of as self-evidently true for philosophy as those of Euclid were then thought to be for geometry. But time, instead of confirming his opinion that there could be but one system of philosophy (whether that of Spinoza or anyone else), even as there was but one system of geometry, has on the contrary neatly controverted it with the discovery that there could be many systems of geometry, just as there are many systems of philosophy.

Hegel made a bold attempt to solve the difficulty by identifying the dialectical process of thought with the supposedly dialectical movement of history; but he met with no more success than his numerous predecessors. Facts stubbornly refused to be so ruthlessly conscripted into the ranks of his dialectical battalions. A crack appeared in the gigantic walls of his building which slowly widened until the magnificent edifice split in two, and the halves had to be dismantled and carted away for the construction of more enduring if less imposing structures elsewhere.

Since the starting point of each philosopher was different, his conclusion also was necessarily different, as well as the line of exposition by which the two were connected. Plato has conferred on the philosopher the grandiose title of 'spectator of all time and all existence', but, although he tells him what to see, he does not tell him from where to see it, whether to take a bird's eye view with the transcendentalist or a worm's eye view with the empiricist.

Indian tradition considers all philosophical points of view (*darśanas*) as more or less equally valid, since Reality is ineffable, and therefore susceptible of more than one intellectual interpretation. All that is expected of any such interpretation is that it should help the person who accepts it to experience for himself the Truth which it can indicate but which it is powerless to describe. Here philosophy and religion meet. But in the West, where the intellect has generally been regarded as making a fully adequate conceptual representation of Reality, the truth of one system precludes the possibility of any other system being true. The question of any pragmatic reference did not, until the days of William James, even arise. Philosophy was one thing and religion another, and the nature of the connection between them remained a matter of uncertainty, except of course to Hegel, who crushed religion on the Procrustean bed of his dialectic as merrily as he had stretched physics. System therefore succeeded system, as century followed century, and one shaky building was put up after another so that, if today we glance backward in history, the philosophical landscape appears dotted with ruins of innumerable structures of all shapes and sizes – melancholy monuments to the pride of human intellect, which would seat knowledge in the chair of wisdom, and elevate mind to the throne of spirit.

Buddhist philosophy (and religion, for the two are inseparable and should always go together and be called *Dharma*) adopts, however, an altogether different procedure, declaring that the only possible religio-philosophical starting-point is not a thought, an idea, or a concept at all, but on the contrary, a feeling, the feeling of pain, physical and mental suffering, *duḥkha*. Nor are we given a merely theoretical definition of pain, for, silently pointing to the solid and incontrovertible facts of birth, old age, disease, death, being separated from those we love, having to live with those we hate, Buddhism lets them speak to us for themselves, and they whisper in the depths of our hearts the tidings that 'all this is pain.'

This shifting of emphasis from the cognitive to the affective modes of experience marks a change in philosophy even more radical than that brought about by the famous 'Copernican Revolution' of Kant, since it brings both philosophy and religion home to 'men's business and bosoms' with an immediacy of impact such as no conceptual commonplace could possibly have achieved. Pain is the common ground whereon meet prince and peasant, mill-hand and millionaire, male and female, old and young, animal and vegetable, man and amoeba. Sentient existence is a great brotherhood of suffering. The same nerves that transmit sensations of pleasure can transmit sensations of pain. If it is the faith of Wordsworth that 'every flower enjoys the air it breathes', it is equally the faith of the Buddhist that every blade of grass 'feels with pain the sting of rain'. Whether we go up or down in the scale of sentient existence, backwards or forwards in time, inward into mind or outward into matter, where there is sensibility there is suffering, and without sensibility life as we know it cannot exist.

Suffering stands out in human life as clearly as the snow peaks of the Himalayas against the cloudless blue autumn sky. Only our infatuation with transitory pleasures prevents us from seeing the fact steadily and whole. Even when we ignore the existence of pain we tacitly admit that it is there, and the more studiously we ignore it, the more damning does the admission become, until one day we are violently torn from whatever pleasure we are clinging to, and confronted with the fearful visage which we had avoided for so long. Even the conceiving of pain as 'the sense of limitation' or 'the feeling of finitude', useful though these variants may be for some purposes, is only too often an attempt to gloss over the uncomfortable fact of suffering. Pain is pain, the pain of a cut on the finger, of a kick on the shins, or a knife in the back or a bullet in the chest, or smoke in the eyes or mustard gas in the lungs; the pain of tooth-ache or stomach-ache; the pain of a wife's infidelity or a friend's ingratitude, of a parent's lack of understanding or a child's indifference; the pain of not getting what you want to get; of losing what you don't want to lose – all this is pain, a feeling not a concept, something to be immediately experienced, not something to be thought about. And this is where Buddhism begins. It would be impossible for it to begin anywhere else.

Although philosophers themselves may be unaware of the fact, all philosophizing begins with the experience of pain, even though philosophical systems may not do so. Buddhism solves the problem of where philosophical exposition is to begin by identifying the psychological starting-point of philosophical activity itself with the logical starting-point of philosophical exposition. Philosophy and religion must begin with pain because that is where philosophizing begins. In fact, it is where all the most important activities of life begin. Men philosophize for the same reason they eat and drink, make love and marry, write books, paint pictures, go on journeys, commit murder and suicide, cheat and steal, work and play – because they feel dissatisfied with their present mode of existence, their immediate experiences; and this feeling of dissatisfaction is what we call pain.

Mankind progresses for the same reason that the amoeba evolves – from irritation. There was never any flower of human achievement but some great sorrow lay at its root. The discovery of this fact, so fearfully obvious yet so flagrantly ignored, together with the recognition of all the momentous consequences which stem therefrom, was a stroke of philosophical genius of the first magnitude, and one which certainly could never have been achieved save by cognition of an altogether supernormal kind, it being the first work of nothing less than Enlightenment itself to proclaim to the world the Noble Truth of the Universality of Suffering.

Here the old charge of pessimism (a term for which there is, significantly enough, no Indian equivalent), trumped up against Buddhism ever since it became known in the West, is usually dragged in, and to the same oft-repeated question, the same almost equally oft-repeated answer must be made. 'Is Buddhism pessimistic?' If, by pessimism, we mean the simple recognition that there are ugly facts and uncomfortable experiences in life, then Buddhism may with justice be described as pessimistic, and not Buddhism alone, but every religion that is not content to be a mere mythology of hopefulness, and every man and woman who is prepared frankly to admit the existence of facts which are experienced by all. But if by pessimism we mean the bleak doctrine that there is no way of mitigating the evil of life, that existence is irredeemably bad, and that the next best thing to not being born is to die quickly, then Buddhism is most emphatically not pessimistic. It could be called pessimistic (though only in the first sense in which we used that term) if it stopped short at the First Noble Truth. Even then it would not be untrue, but only partially true. But, since Buddhism goes on to enunciate the Second Truth of the Cause of Suffering, the Third Truth of its Cessation, and the Fourth Truth of the Way to its Cessation, it is with the grossest injustice that it can be described as pessimistic. Problems are never solved by ignoring them. The frank recognition of a difficulty is the first step towards overcoming it. As well call a doctor a pessimist because he diagnoses the disease of a patient whom he wishes to cure as describe Buddhism as pessimistic because it recognizes the existence of the suffering it intends to remove.

It is easy, though, to make the mistake that Buddhism is concerned only with the removal of suffering, and it is a mistake which certain Buddhists frequently make. Just as the particular kind of pain incidental to bodily existence is a symptom of physical ill-health, so is the wider and more inclusive pain of existence itself a sign that there is something radically wrong with life as a whole. In both cases we are confronted not simply with the straightforward task of relieving pain, but also with the infinitely more difficult and complex one of readjusting the unbalanced somatic or psychological condition which is its cause, thus rendering the patient physically or spiritually healthy, hale, and whole.

Suffering is important, not for its own sake, but because it is a sign that we are not living as we ought to live. Buddhism does not encourage morbid obsession with suffering as though it were the be-all and end-all of existence. What we really have to get rid of is not suffering but the imperfection which suffering warns us is there, and in the course of getting rid of imperfection and attaining perfection we may have to accept, paradoxically enough, the experience of suffering as indispensable to the achievement of final success. True it is that by the experience of pain we are compelled to enter upon the Path, and true it is that when we arrive at the Goal there will be no more pain; but if we think that following the Path means nothing more than the studious avoidance of painful experiences we are making a mistake of astronomical dimensions, and plunging headlong down the path of a spiritual selfishness so utterly diabolical that it is frightful to contemplate even the idea of it.

The essence of Buddhism consists not in the removal of suffering, which is only negative and incidental, but in the attainment of perfection, which is positive and fundamental. The Bodhisattva is not afraid of suffering. He accepts it joyfully if he thinks it will assist him to the attainment of his great goal of 'Enlightenment for the sake of all sentient beings'. The Christian mystic would continue to love God even though cast down into Hell, for he loves God for His own sake, not for the sake of any reward, not even for happiness (though he is not unhappy, for love is happiness). It is only the spiritual individualist, the typical Hīnayānist of Buddhist tradition, who 'loves' God for the sake of escaping the pains of Hell. Not for our own sakes, not even for the sake of 'others', should we attain the Divine, but simply and solely for its own irresistible sake.

The fact that Buddhism takes as its starting point not a concept but a feeling, has not only a philosophical but also a religious significance. It solves at one stroke a problem of methodology and a problem of practical spiritual living. It is a well-known fact, and one to which we have alluded more than once in our writings, that the theoretical understanding of religious doctrines is one thing, the practical application and realization of them, quite another. 'Five Latin words', says Aldous Huxley, 'sum up the moral history of every man and woman who has ever lived:

Video meliora proboque
Deteriora sequor.
(I see the better and approve it; the worse is what I pursue). [9]

If in truth Man was a rational animal, as the philosophers of the eighteenth century believed he was, knowing would be indistinguishable from doing, understanding equivalent to practising. But he is, on the contrary, a desiderative animal, a creature of desires, like any other animal, except that in his case the great root feelings of love and hatred (in the sense of attraction to pleasant and repulsion from painful experiences) have branched out into innumerable derivative forms called emotions. [10] And since it is his desires, his experience of pleasure and pain, which ultimately determine his behaviour, it is only by somehow appealing to and utilizing them that human behaviour can be influenced and changed. Most of all must religion, which seeks to work in human nature the most radical of all possible changes, be able not only to scratch the rational surface but also to penetrate the desiderative depths of the psyche.

By beginning with the fact of pain Buddhism involves the whole emotional nature of man from the very onset. Recognition of the First Noble Truth comes not as a pleasant intellectual diversion but as a terrible emotional shock. The Scriptures say that one feels then like a man who suddenly realizes that his turban is in flames. Only a shock of this kind is strong enough to galvanize the whole being into action. The most astonishing intellectual discovery is no more than an agreeable titillation in the region of the cerebral hemispheres. Only when a man feels strongly will he act effectively. It is for this reason above all others that Buddhism starts not with a concept but with a feeling, not with intellectual postulation but with emotional experience. Perhaps it is for this reason that the spiritual dynamism and creativeness of Buddhism have never been exhausted; it has flowered again and again through the ages, growing not weaker but stronger, not withered but more fresh and beautiful, as the years passed and the centuries flew by on silent wings. And if there is to be in this century, as it seems reasonable to surmise, a particularly glorious efflorescence of the religion of the Enlightened One, it will be made possible only by the correct and thorough understanding of where Buddhism begins, and why it begins there.

The Flowering Bowl

It is one of the postulates of modern educational theory that the mother-tongue of the student – that is to say, the vehicle of communication most natural to him – should be the medium of instruction from the earliest to the latest stages of his scholastic career. Nor is the application of this principle to be confined to the sphere of secular learning, since it exercises jurisdiction with equal authority over the domain of sacred learning, of what is commonly called 'religion', but has in India been known from ancient times as *dharma*, and that which modern Western writers, dissatisfied with the connotation of the word religion, now prefer to term Tradition.

That 'Every man should learn the Doctrine in his own language' is a precept which the Buddha not only laid down with the utmost clarity (the occasion being when some of His Brahmin disciples approached Him for permission to render His teachings into Sanskrit verses) but which He also illustrated most abundantly in practice by preaching in the vernaculars of His time. Hence the unparalleled activity of the Buddhist missionaries in making translations and hence the prodigious bulk of Buddhist sacred literature in Pali, Sanskrit, Tibetan, Chinese, Mongolian, and Japanese. A bulk which, if it possesses the disadvantage of bewildering the brain of the modern scholar with its sheer interminability – wave upon wave of books rising up and deluging him from this veritable ocean of literature – has nevertheless had the compensating advantage of preventing the growth of that bibliolatrous attitude of mind which springs up only too rapidly within the more circumscribed compass of a narrower range of authoritative texts.

The word 'language' should not, however, be understood as limited to the expression of thoughts and desires in verbal form. A perfectly legitimate extension of its meaning enables it to include not only thoughts and desires unexpressed in words, but all those systems of thought and patterns of emotion which have been built up from them, by a process of gradual elaboration, as well. It is for this reason possible to speak of music as 'the language of the soul' and as 'the universal language'. By 'language' is here meant simply a medium by which the soul's rarest intuitions and most delicate nuances of feeling, in the first place, and experiences common to all members of the human family, in the second, are able to find expression.

It is, moreover, possible for us to speak of the whole body of human culture, with its various limbs of philosophy, the sciences, the arts, education, and so on, as being the language of humanity; the single continuous expression of the human spirit in terms of space and time, as the several 'parts', in fact, of the one 'speech' of man's earthly utterance. The way in which men dress, the kind of houses in which they live, the make and shape of their articles of domestic use, their manners and their social customs, are all so many minor languages, so many revelations of themselves, so many signs which are, to the eye of understanding, as intelligible as a row of words on the printed page.

But what is it precisely, one may legitimately enquire, that finds expression in the culture of humanity in the same way that the thoughts and desires of individual men and women find utterance in human speech? If culture and civilization parallel the Word, what is there behind them which parallels the Idea?

Where what have aptly been termed 'traditional' cultures and civilizations are concerned, the question admits of a simple and straightforward answer: Tradition itself is what finds expression, with varying degrees of clarity and vigour of utterance, through all the diversity of their outward modes. Tradition means primarily that Transcendent Knowledge gained by the Wise and by Them transmitted to Their disciples, and by these to their own pupils in uninterrupted 'apostolic' succession; secondarily, the Doctrine in which, for the purpose of universal dissemination, that Knowledge finds more or less adequate metaphysical formulation; and, thirdly, all those 'religious' disciplines and 'spiritual' practices by means of which the Doctrine is to be understood and the Knowledge realized. Traditional cultures or civilizations are those which are vehicles for Tradition – whether in its Hindu, Buddhist, Christian, Muslim, or Taoist-Confucian forms – and which, through the multiplicity of the philosophies, arts, sciences, political systems, and social conventions which pertain to them, communicate in due order the traditional Methods, Doctrine, and Knowledge to the men and women who are born within their respective folds. In a traditional civilization, not only is it true that

An old pine-tree preaches wisdom,
And a wild bird is crying out Truth,

but even the design of a cup, or the pattern of a plate, a minor social custom no less than a major philosophical doctrine – may serve as the means whereby a man is reminded (and reminded the more often the more closely the thread of the support concerned is woven into the texture of his daily life) of that Transcendent Knowledge which is the goal of human existence, the alone Desirable, the truly Fair.

It is for this reason that the normative life is so much easier to live in a traditional civilization than in one which is non-traditional or even anti-traditional. It may without any exaggeration be said that it would be more profitable spiritually to be a layman in the former kind of society than to be a monk or a priest in either of the latter. A Hindu peasant or a Tibetan Buddhist muleteer is often better acquainted with the Doctrine and Methods of his Tradition than is an English archdeacon or an American bishop with those of that to which they both nominally belong.

When Buddhism overflowed the boundaries of India and poured into the surrounding Asian countries it was but natural that those life-giving waters should irrigate the fields of the hearts and minds of their inhabitants through the emotional and intellectual channels already formed there by habits and customs centuries old. Just as a man who goes to live in a foreign country learns its language, so did Buddhism acquire the language of the countries to which its beneficent influence spread, and this not only in the narrow verbal sense but also in the immeasurably wider sense to which reference has already been made.

The Transcendent Knowledge, the Doctrine, and the methods of the Indian Buddhist Tradition found new and rich expression through the peculiar social institutions and distinctive aesthetic forms of China, Japan, Tibet, and other lands. The soil wherefrom the great tree of Buddhism grew may have been rich or poor, the flowers which it produced, red or white or blue in colour, but the Seed from which it germinated, and the flavour of the Fruit which it ultimately bore, were always one.

The history of Buddhist art, wherein the figure of the Buddha Himself, in any one of its innumerably varied poses, occupies the central place, affords one of the most obvious and pleasing illustrations of this process. As the Buddha-image and the Buddha-icon spread slowly to the North, South, and East, from the place of their origin, a gradual transformation in their bodily proportions, and their dress, took place. If the images of Gandhāra, with their rounded facial contours and graceful draperies, are reminiscent of the Grecian Apollo, the frescoes of Ajantā reveal a typical young Indian prince with all the sinuous beauty of his race; while those of China convey the sense of homely mysteriousness which might belong to an ideal Taoist sage. The Buddhas of Burma and Mongolia, of Ceylon and Nepal, are no less natives of the lands which they inhabit, and faithfully reflect in their tranquil faces the features of their worshippers, thereby giving weight to Voltaire's flippant epigram that 'God created man in His own image, and man returned the compliment.'

Such transformations as these are sometimes of great doctrinal significance. The sedent figure of the Indian Buddha, for instance, with eyes half closed and His begging-bowl in his lap, often undergoes a curious modification when depicted on the marvellous painted 'banners' (*thangkas*) of Tibet. The bowl, which Indian art leaves empty, in these Tibetan paintings often contains a ball of rice or a nosegay of flowers. While the first variation on the sacred theme may simply reflect the average Tibetan's extremely concrete and practical approach to the things of his Tradition, the second seems to suggest a deepened insight into the meaning of the symbol itself which merits more than a casual reference.

The bhikṣu or Buddhist monk was originally, and still is, to a certain extent, a mendicant; one who, for the sake of being able to devote every minute of his time and every ounce of his energy to the attainment of the supreme end of human existence, renounced all worldly pursuits, including that of earning his livelihood, and depended for the satisfaction of his bodily needs solely upon what the faithful dropped into his bowl when once a day he went from door to door in quest of alms. The begging-bowl of the Buddhist monk may therefore be considered, ethically speaking, as a symbol of renunciation, although the renunciation here contemplated is, so far as it goes, outward and superficial rather than inward and profound, an observance more than an attitude of mind, and therefore pertaining rather to Method than to Knowledge. (This is not to under-estimate its value, however, as some hasty moderns might suppose, since, in the words of Lao Tze, 'A journey of a thousand miles starts with a single step', and in every educational system the way to the higher grades lies inescapably through the lower ones.)

When, however, renunciation is considered as belonging not merely to the ethical, but as operative in the intellectual and spiritual orders as well – when, that is to say, it is more deeply understood as the transcending of all dualistic concepts and separative movements of the will – then the empty begging-bowl of conventional mendicancy becomes the symbol of absolute spiritual poverty, of complete conceptual nakedness, of utter self-deprivation – in a word, of Śūnyatā, the voidness, itself.

It was perhaps due to the predominantly cognitive character of the genius of Indian Buddhism that it stressed so emphatically, particularly in its Śūnyavāda form, that Reality which transcends absolutely all the categories of our understanding, for ever towering with implacable and terrifying otherness above every conceptual limitation that we seek to impose upon it. Of this phase of Enlightenment, wherein is annihilated every vestige of ideation, the empty begging-bowl of the mendicant monk is a fitting symbol.

But when Buddhism penetrated northward across the mountain barriers of the Himalaya and began to inhale the bracing air of the lofty Tibetan plateau, a gradual shifting of emphasis occurred. The virile and energetic genius of the Tibetan people was not fully satisfied by a simply negative representation of the content of Enlightenment, and before long their innate spiritual athleticism succeeded in educing therefrom some of its more positive and dynamic elements.

The Compassion Aspect of the Buddha-Nature was emphasized and received a novel development in the doctrine of the *tulkus* or *nirmāṇakāyas* of various Bodhisattvas, of whom Avalokiteśvara, the Patron of Tibet, is the most prominent. The Tibetan yogis revelled in the experience of the Power Aspect of Enlightenment, and portrayed it in their sacred art under numberless vigorous and fearful forms. When studying the Tibetan religious genius one is struck by its consciousness of and delight in the unbounded Compassion and inexhaustible Energy which stream forth from the bosom of Reality. That which appears as darkness and stillness to the eye of the conceptual understanding is to their glad vision full of sonorous light. Of this dynamic aspect of Reality, within whose apparent emptiness spring up exuberantly transcendent Wisdom, Love, and Power, the flowering bowl which Tibetan art places in the hands of the Buddha is a not inappropriate symbol.

It should not be thought that such a development in any way constitutes a deviation from the Doctrines and Methods of the original Indian Tradition. What the Indian gurus transmitted to their Tibetan pupils was, fundamentally, the experience of Enlightenment, and while this element of the traditional complex remains constant and unchanged in the Tibetan as in every other branch of Buddhism, the Doctrines and Methods by which it was mediated, and which are its supports and instruments, were emphasized here and adapted there in accordance with the spiritual requirements of the Tibetan people. The Buddhism of Tibet has not planted flowers in the Buddha's bowl, but simply provided conditions suitable for the germination of seeds that were there from the beginning.

If the figure of the Buddha is understood as the symbol of Reality as it exists beyond all conceptual determinations, positive as well as negative, the Flowering Bowl (not merely, be it noted, the bowl *containing* flowers) which he holds in His hands may be regarded as the symbol of the dual determinations which we are compelled to superimpose upon It – that of the Wisdom of the voidness and that of Compassionate Activity, which an alternative symbolism represents statically as being in a state of inseparable Union, and which our symbolism represents dynamically, the one springing up inexhaustibly in exuberant efflorescence from the other.

The Diamond Path

The doctrine that the conception of a separate soul, self, or ego-entity is illusory forms, negatively speaking, the ultimate plinth and foundation of the entire vast superstructure of Buddhist philosophy and religion. Every single precept of ethical behaviour, each prescribed method of meditation and higher spiritual practice, is directed towards the eradication of that sense of separateness which seeks to build up 'narrow domestic walls' between its own small individual life and the vast universal life which flows on all around it. Nothing in the material or spiritual universe exists in complete, or really even in partial, isolation from the remainder of that all-embracing whole of existence of which it is so integrally a part, and to shut one's eyes to this supremely important fact – the positive expression of the negative doctrine of *anattā* or selflessness – is deliberately to deprive oneself of that insight into the mutuality and interpenetratingness of all things which is simultaneously the secret of liberating Wisdom and of redeeming Compassion.

> *Nothing in this world is single,*
> *All things, by a law divine,*
> *In one another's being mingle,…*

sang the poet Shelley in a moment of inspiration. Every individual thing in the universe continually transcends the limitations of its own individuality by reflecting in the depths of its being the image of every other living thing in the universe. The very content of its own 'individuality' cries out against the lie that it is alone. By the very mouth of selfhood is blabbed the secret of selflessness. It was not merely in hyperbole that the poet-seer spoke of seeing the world in a grain of sand, heaven in a wild flower, the universe in the palm of his hand, and eternity in an hour, but with all the stark literalness of real mystic experience. The highest things are reflected in the lowest, just as the lowest are in their turn reflected in the Highest. Nirvāṇa or Buddhahood is reflected in the heart of every sentient being as the *Tathāgatadhātu* or Element of Buddhahood, in the development of which to the utmost limit of its potentialities the career of the Bodhisattva essentially consists. Similarly, the ignorance and suffering of all sentient beings are mirrored in the very heart of Enlightenment, which is the philosophical explanation of why the Bodhisattva even after his 'Nirvāṇa' continues to work for the salvation of the world. All things in the universe are, in the philosophico-poetical language of Aśvaghoṣa, perfumed as it were with Suchness (the ontological aspect of Nirvāṇa or Buddhahood) just as a garment is made fragrant by the intangible scent of flowers. Every single thing in the universe, however mean or insignificant it may outwardly seem, bears deep within itself as the truest and most essential part of its being the trace of absolute purity and perfection. This is the famous Jewel which the great Sanskrit mantra *oṁ maṇi padme hūṁ*, so beloved of the people of Tibet, informs us lies hidden in what is, microcosmically speaking, the heart-lotus of every being, and what is, macrocosmically speaking, the world-lotus of mundane existence itself.

Thus it is possible to analyse every single object in the universe into an Absolute, Nirvāṇic, or perfect aspect, and a relative, Saṁsāric, or imperfect aspect. In Tantric Buddhism the former is often spoken of as the Vajra or Diamond aspect of existence. Everything possesses a Diamond or Noumenal aspect corresponding to its material or phenomenal aspect. Corresponding to the simple earthly flower springing up from the soil there is a transcendental Diamond Flower, which is that aspect of the flower in which it is perfumed by, or in which it reflects and is reflected by, the reality of Suchness. Similarly, as the transcendental aspect of our fickle and unsteady mundane mind there exists the mind which is 'pure and hard as flaming diamond', the *Vajracitta* – human personality in its highest possible aspect of freeness, mutuality, and interpenetratingness with regard to all other things in the universe. That highest and most real aspect of existence in which everything interpenetrates every other thing, and wherein everything reflects, and is in turn reflected by, every other phenomenon (offering no obstruction to each other whatsoever, like the mutual interpenetration of innumerable beams of coloured light), is called the *Dharmadhātu*, the Realm of Truth, or the *Vajradhātu*, the Diamond World. The Bodhisattva aspires to live in this world, the world of realities, instead of in that presented by the ordinary mundane consciousness, the world of illusions. This does not mean that he tries to run away from this world to some other world supposed to be existing on the other side of the universe. The so-called objective universe exists only in relation to our own minds: it would be more correct to say that the world exists in us than we in it. Consequently, real change of place can be effected only by a radical change of mind, that is to say, by a transformation in the state of consciousness of the subject. The Bodhisattva transports himself from the realm of mundane existence to the Realm of Truth, the Diamond World, by realizing that the two worlds are in reality one world, and that all he has to do is to give up perceiving things in their illusory aspect of separate mutually exclusive realities, and to learn instead to perceive them in their Absolute or Diamond aspect as the parts of a perfectly interpenetrating Whole.

The spiritual life does not consist, as it is so often mistakenly supposed to do, in the mere denial of, or flight from, the things of the 'world' to the things of the 'spirit', as though the latter stood over against the other or looked down upon them with a fierce scowl of irreconcilable opposition. This kind of attitude results only in repression and in all the evils which are inevitably attendant upon repression. All systems of spiritual culture which are founded upon a dualistic philosophy ultimately create a split in the psyche, with the result that the total energy of the individual is expended in the exhausting struggles which are continually taking place between the 'higher' and 'lower' aspects of personality, instead of being devoted exclusively to the realization of Nirvāṇa. The problem of the spiritual life is essentially dynamic. It consists not in the understanding of spiritual truths, but in integrating the dissipated psychic energies of the individual for achieving the realization of these truths. The Tantric Buddhist system of spiritual culture, being founded upon a non-dualistic (though this does not mean upon a monistic) philosophy, neither creates conflict in the psyche nor dissipates its psychic energies. It teaches the devotee neither to fight with nor to fly from mundane things, but simply to view them in their Absolute or diamond aspect. The Bodhisattva should feel that he is really all the time living in the Realm of Truth, the Diamond World, and that it is only the blindness of his ignorance which prevents him from realizing this fact. He should try to view all the important relationships and experiences of life in their noumenal aspect, feeling, even though he cannot clearly perceive, that the mundane things in the midst of which he lives and moves and has his being are simply the ghostly shadows of these bright realities which collectively make up the Diamond World of perfect mutual interpenetration. However gross the relationship, however mundane the experience, the Bodhisattva knows that the Diamond aspect of it is there all the time, and upon this he therefore seeks to direct his gaze. This he strives to develop and cultivate so that it gradually absorbs all the psychic energies which were formerly sucked in by its mundane counterpart.

The Tantric Buddhist religious discipline has not hesitated to cultivate in this way even the relationship which in its lowest form is based upon sexual desire. Instead of denouncing sexual relations as sinful and demanding the complete inhibition of sexual feeling, it exhorts the aspirant to understand and develop the transcendental or Diamond aspect of these relations and feelings. Even in ordinary sexual desire there is often present a quality of self-sacrifice or self-abnegation which helps to sanctify it. If this aspect of the relation in question is cultivated, the creative energies usually absorbed in the gratification of desire will be liberated in the direction of self-transcendence. This is not for one moment to suggest that the Tantric Buddhist teaching in its purity encourages the physical gratification of sexual desire. It merely states the way in which that desire, and even the act of its physical gratification, can be dealt with when it happens to be present, or chances to occur, so as to make ultimately for liberation instead of for bondage. A famous Tantric Buddhist verse declares that the yogi is liberated by those very practices by which others are bound. It is important to remember, however, that such practices liberate him only to the extent that he succeeds in cultivating the element of self-transcendence which they contain, and bind him to the extent that he merely enjoys the element of self-indulgence like any ordinary mortal. A love-relation which involves sensuous gratification of any sort can carry the aspirant along only the most elementary stages of the Diamond Path. But a passion intense and pure as that of Dante for Beatrice involves such an immense concentration of psychic energy that when the phenomenal aspect of the loved person is swallowed up in the transcendental Diamond aspect, this concentration of energy is released with a velocity so tremendous that the whole personality of the lover is lifted up and carried far within the boundaries of the Diamond World. It will be noted that in this system of spiritual discipline love-relation with another human being, not with a mythological personage or imaginary deity, is sought to be cultivated. For in common with all other schools of Buddhism the Tantric tradition considers the conception of an anthropomorphic creator-god to be a delusion, and hence a source of bondage, so that no practice based upon belief in the truth of this delusion can be a source of liberation.

Another emotionally rich and important sphere of human activity and experience is the aesthetic. It has been recognized even in the West (by Schopenhauer) that all great art contains an element of self-transcendence akin to that which constitutes the quintessence of religion. When this element of self-transcendence is consciously cultivated in poetry, in music, or in painting and sculpture, instead of the element of mere sensuous appeal, art ceases to be a form of sensuous indulgence and becomes a kind of spiritual discipline, and the highest stages of aesthetic contemplation become spiritual experiences. This is, perhaps, the chief reason for the truly tropical iconographical richness of Tantric Buddhism. A system of spiritual culture aiming at the concentration and canalization of emotion, which is the precious life-blood equally of religion and of art, and which moreover professes to develop the transcendental aspect of every variety of human experience, can hardly fail to be applied to such a vast and legitimate sphere of its activity as that of the fine arts.

The sphere of love-relation and aesthetic experience are but two of all those exploited in the interests of the religious life by the Tantric Buddhist system of spiritual culture, a system which aims at revealing the transcendental aspect of every phenomenon of human consciousness, and which thereby seeks to disengage the psychic energies from the multiplicity of empirical objects over which they are normally dissipated and to liberate them in the direction of Enlightenment. But these two important examples are sufficient to illustrate in a general way the spiritual alchemy by which the dross of mundane experience is transmuted into the pure gold of transcendental experience and intuition. Through this alchemy the Great Work of Enlightenment is accomplished, and the Bodhisattva traverses within the depths of his own mind the Diamond Path which leads from the mundane world of separative and mutually exclusive existences to the Realm of Truth, the Diamond World, the world of the perfect mutuality and interpenetration of all things.

GETTING BEYOND THE EGO

ALMOST ALL RELIGIONS HAVE RECOGNIZED, albeit with varying degrees of emphasis, that the eradication of egoism, or the illusory sense of separative selfhood, is the central and most essential task of any genuinely spiritual life. From the most primitive tribal taboos to the most highly developed systems of altruistic ethics their function is one and the same: to curb and gradually to eliminate that instinct of self-assertion which is, in gross or subtle form, the principal characteristic of all grades of sentient existence.

Some religious teachings, such as those of original Christianity and Islam, but dimly perceived, and then only in its darker shades and more tangible aspects, the mighty and mysterious workings of the peril-fraught sense of separative selfhood; while another teaching, like Buddhism in all its branches, has turned the searchlight of its enquiry on to its finest and whitest forms, mercilessly exposing its subtlest expressions and delicatest nuances.

All can recognize for what it is the coarse egoism which fights and struggles to possess material things, or the slightly less coarse egoism that craves for power, praise, or fame; but to few indeed is given that piercing eagle vision which can discern the egoism lurking in the desire for eternal life, or in the longing for communion with some personal god.

In accordance with the superficiality or profundity of its understanding of the extent to which egoism dominates and controls human life, so are the prescriptions for its elimination which are given by a religious teaching more or less radical in character. Some are satisfied with the renunciation of the cruder forms of lust and hatred, such as murder, theft, and adultery, but tolerate and even approve the more refined forms of these same separative passions, such as the craving for immortality, or the belief in some ghostly 'higher' selfhood which is supposedly more real than the 'lower' kind. Buddhism, however, is satisfied with nothing less than the absolute renunciation of the ego-sense in its subtlest no less than in its grossest formulations, and with the all-compelling mantra of *anattā* exorcizes even the most tenuous spectre of selfhood.

But so much at least is clear: that the true spiritual aspirant, to whatever religious denomination he may belong, finds himself confronted from the very beginning with the problem of eliminating the sense of separative selfhood, and finds, moreover, that certain means, certain spiritual practices, are available to him for this purpose. He may devote himself to prayer, meditation, or philanthropic works, with the hope of eliminating his selfish desires and becoming completely selfless in thought, word, and deed. He may flagellate his body or fast, he may observe a vow of silence, or, like St Simeon Stylites, he may spend his life squatting on the top of a pillar. He may read the lives of saints, or give in charity to the poor, or pass many silent days and nights in exalted states of superconsciousness. And it will seem as though his ego-sense was becoming attenuated. But if we look closely into his state of consciousness we will find that without exception it takes the form of 'I am fasting', 'I am praying', 'I am meditating', or even 'I have attained'. We find, in other words, that the ego-sense has not been eliminated, but that it has simply been dissociated from 'worldly' activities and associated with 'religious' activities. The net result is almost the same. The ego functions with full force and in fact all the more dangerously for that its presence and activity are not perceived.

Here we encounter in its acutest form the central problem of the spiritual, as distinct from the merely religious, life. The ego-sense, the sense of separative selfhood, together with all those blind movements of attraction and repulsion which it inevitably involves, is to be eliminated, and certain practices are available for that purpose; but the ego-sense, instead of being eliminated thereby, simply transfers itself to those very practices which were intended to annihilate it. Like an unwanted but faithful dog, it is kicked out of the front door only to creep in at the back. Herein lies the tragedy of many a spiritual life. The more we struggle to eliminate our ego-sense the subtler and stronger and more dangerous it becomes. We revolve within a vicious circle from which there seems to be no possibility of escape. The man who thinks 'I am enlightened' is equally far from Nirvāṇa as the man who thinks 'I am rich.' The saint may be more attached to his sanctity than the sinner to his sin. In fact, a 'good' man's core of separative selfhood is often harder and more impenetrable to the Infinite Light of Amitābha than that of a 'bad' man shattered into humility and repentance by the consciousness of his sinful deeds.

What, then, is the way out of the difficulty? Certainly not by ceasing from activities, for that is impossible for beings whose very stuff is flux and change. The choice which we are called upon to make is never between action and inaction, but only between one action and another, and ultimately between egoistic and non-egoistic or empty actions. But what actions are non-egoistic or empty? Are there such actions, and how are we to recognize them? We have already seen that any action, however holy or altruistic it may outwardly seem, may be smirched and tainted by the sense of separative selfhood. The very radicalness of the difficulty provides the key to its own solution. We are not to imagine that we have to look for any separate class or kind of non-egoistic activities, for the fact that the ego-sense may attach itself to any action has already precluded that possibility; but we have simply to change our attitude towards our action. We have to act without the sense of 'I' or 'mine'. This is not nearly so easy as it sounds. The problem of inaction (which is what non-egoistic action amounts to karmically) has to be solved in the very midst of action. Activity must stream forth from the very heart of emptiness.

But by what practical method or by what spiritual discipline are we to eliminate that sense of 'I'-ness which seems to cling fast to everything we do, dragging it down into the mire of selfhood and besmirching even the skirts of sanctity? The question tacitly reverts to that very attitude which is productive of the problem of non-egoistic action. We do not have to take up any method or discipline, we do not have to perform any new action, but simply to change our attitude to what we are already doing, to act without the egoistic consciousness of acting.

The non-egoistic attitude assumes two principal forms. In the first, all activities are attributed to the Other, and the subject confesses his utter inability to perform any action whatsoever, whether good or bad. This is the devotional form of the non-egoistic attitude. Herein the devotee surrenders himself body and soul to the object of his adoration. In the second form of the non-egoistic attitude the practitioner simply watches himself as he performs the various actions of life, whether sacred or profane, and constantly bears in mind that they are all egoless and empty, that there is action but no actor, deed but no doer. This is the more intellectual form of the non-egoistic attitude. By these two methods the ego-sense is gradually attenuated. But although the first or devotional form of the non-egoistic attitude is able to eliminate the grosser kinds of egoism it is not able to eliminate the subtler kinds, for the subject stands irreducibly over against the Object to the very end, and it is therefore necessary to have recourse to the second or more intellectual method if the elimination of the ego-sense is to be complete. Moreover, the idea of the Other is usually that of a more or less anthropomorphic deity, usually credited with the creation of the world, and to whom only good qualities are generally attributed. This raises several theological difficulties, such as the origin of evil, and since the devotee naturally shrinks from attributing his sinful actions to the deity his renunciation of his actions cannot be carried to its logical extreme, and he is compelled to confess that the sinful actions at least are his own. Consequently, recourse to the other form of the non-egoistic attitude, wherein no such difficulties arise, is sooner or later inevitable. The sense of all-pervading emptiness is the only key to non-egoistic action.

When this point is arrived at the practitioner realizes that it is not necessary to perform any 'religious' action, but that those actions are in the deepest and truest sense religious wherein is no sense of agency, no feeling that 'I am the doer'. It should not be supposed, however, that this doctrine countenances any form of antinomianism. We have said elsewhere that although emptiness or egolessness transcends the purely empirical distinction between moral good and evil it nevertheless expresses itself in the field of life and action in a determinate manner as a moral, not as an immoral, activity, and that the very essence of this activity is compassion. It is impossible that a man who is fully Enlightened, that is to say, who is absolutely empty of selfhood, should be able, as some sects teach, to kill or to steal, to commit the sexual act or to tell lies. Those who assert that the trans-moral superman or 'living-free' (*jīvanmukta*) may act indifferently either in a moral or an immoral manner are simply fashioning a philosophical cloak for their own ethical nakedness. The activity of emptiness is ever serene and harmonious, and appears in the world as a beneficial force fighting on the side of the good for the ultimate triumph of truth and righteousness. That is why the Jewel of Transcendental Wisdom, the *Vajracchedikā Prajñāpāramitā Sūtra*, says that the Bodhisattva engages himself in the salvation of all sentient beings at the same time that he realizes that there are no sentient beings for him to save. The spiritual life is in the highest sense purposeless.

Although the criterion of the spirituality of any action consists in the presence or absence of ego-sense, there is a class of actions which are inseparably connected with the ego-sense, or which are simply the outward forms or expressions of that sense, and which it would be a contradiction in terms to speak of as being performed egolessly. With the exception of this class of actions (to which belong killing, stealing, unchastity, and falsehood), every one of which is to be completely eschewed, all actions are to be performed with full mindfulness of their essentially empty and egoless nature. As this sense of universal emptiness and egolessness gradually deepens it will begin to vibrate, as it were, and flashes of compassion will dart forth with greater and greater frequency. Beneficial activities for the sake of all sentient beings will spontaneously manifest themselves. But these compassionate activities, also, the practitioner will perceive to be absolutely empty of all selfhood. Even while engaged in the lofty task of universal salvation he will not cherish the illusory idea that he does, nor that there are beings to whom he does, anything at all. The more vivid and intense becomes his realization of emptiness, the more abundant become his compassionate activities for the sake of all sentient beings. Again, the more abundant become his compassionate activities for the sake of all sentient beings, the more vivid and intense becomes his realization of emptiness. In this way the follower of the Buddha solves in his own life the problem of egoless activity.

Those who perform even 'good' actions with the egoistic consciousness of doing good, who appropriate the 'goodness' of an action to themselves, clinging to it and seeking to use it as a badge wherewith to distinguish themselves from others less obviously virtuous, are bound by their 'virtue' to the wheel of birth and death. The more 'good' they do the more tightly they bind themselves and the more they suffer. He only is able to solve the problem of egoless action who constantly remembers that all actions are pure and void of all separative selfhood. He only is able to destroy egoism root and branch who does not claim even the most virtuous action for his 'own'. Such a one alone is able to remain 'inactive' in the midst of action, and to realize that Emptiness-Compassion which is Buddhahood in the midst of this illusory and fleeting world.

The Way of Emptiness

THE MOST CONSPICUOUS THING ABOUT LIFE is that it never remains the same for two consecutive moments; but this lack of persistent identity is a fact to which most people appear perfectly oblivious, if we judge them by their outward behaviour at least.

To the pure mind everything appears as in fact it really is: a process of unceasing flux wherein one thing continually passes over into another, and wherein all things exist in a state of 'unimpeded mutual solution'. In such a state of perfect mutuality there are no lines of demarcation between one individual existence and another: nothing offers any resistance to being penetrated by every other thing; but one individual existence slides smoothly and easily, as it were, into another, each into all, all into each, and all into all, like the unimpeded interpenetration of innumerable beams of light.

The pure mind perceives the world as the Pure Land, the Abode of Bliss (Sukhāvati), the Realm of Truth (Dharmaloka), as the Buddha-field (Buddhakṣetra).

But the mind which is sullied by ignorance and desire strives to arrest the flow, to dam the river of becoming with solid blocks of concepts, to freeze the waves of change into static identities. For the characteristic of ignorance is to perceive things as different, as mutually exclusive, as things-in-themselves; while the characteristic of desire is to grasp one thing and reject another, to seek pleasure and avoid pain, to love self and hate not-self.

The impure mind perceives the world as a World of Desire (kāmaloka) and therefore as a World of suffering (sahāloka). For it is one of the paradoxes of life that none is so certain to experience unhappiness as he who struggles to avoid it.

When the goal of the spiritual life is reached things are seen as they really are, although it should not be supposed that there are two worlds, one of appearance, the other of reality; the two worlds are one world. The means by which the goal is attained is the eradication of ignorance and desire. The spiritual life is nothing but a progressive loosening of the bonds of separative individuality, of selfhood and egoity. Then the universe no longer appears as an unchanging system of static things and rigid relations, but as a delightfully free and fluid interplay of constantly changing terms. It is not so much that reality changes as that reality is change. Spiritual life begins with one's first awakening to this fact.

The individual self is a centre from which lines of discrimination radiate in all directions. It is the innermost citadel of separateness. Only when this centre expands to infinity, only when the walls of this citadel are razed to the ground, is the consummation of the spiritual life achieved.

Liberation is not so much of the self as from the self. He who conceives the spiritual life as a means of attaining eternal bliss has not understood. The whole conception of attainment is fundamentally wrong. One has simply to break down the barriers of his separative individuality and allow himself to be penetrated by everything that exists. Then he will himself penetrate everything. This mutual penetration is liberation, is happiness.

The self is the sole obstacle to the 'attainment' of happiness. Misery is the inseparable shadow of self. And the more solid the substance is, the blacker will its shadow be. To seek happiness is to seek sorrow.

It is another of the paradoxes of life that he only is happy who does not care for happiness.

The spiritual life has no goal. The means is the goal. We do not have to attain anything, but to realize that we have already attained.

To discriminate between the goal and the means, purity and impurity, Enlightenment and non-enlightenment, the Buddha and the debauchee, Nirvāṇa and Saṁsāra, is the work of ignorance. To want to become a Buddha is the surest way of remaining an ordinary man. One may become full of wisdom and charity and may even be able to work miracles, but he will not be a Buddha. To aspire to Nirvāṇa simply strengthens the bonds of desire which bind one to Saṁsāra. For since these terms are all discriminated by ignorance the activities which are based upon them all take place within ignorance and do not succeed in transcending it. The more we strive to be spiritual the more unspiritual we become. The so-called religious life is fundamentally irreligious.

Even if it were possible to 'attain' Buddhahood we should still remain in bondage. For the spiritual life does not consist in the addition of any thing to the ego, however great, however spiritual, that thing may be, but in the subtraction of the ego from all things. Better to pick up a straw from the ground without a sense of ego than to attain Buddhahood with the sense of ego.

Should we, then, abandon our efforts to lead the spiritual life and attain Nirvāṇa? Should we allow ourselves to slip back into the mire of Saṁsāra from which we had so painfully raised ourselves a few inches? No, we should double and treble our efforts; but we should remember that all our efforts are void. We should vow to liberate all beings, to serve all Buddhas, to realize all truths, to eradicate all passions; but we should remember that in reality there are no beings to be liberated, no Buddhas to serve, no truths to realize, no passions to eradicate. To the extent that we realize their essential voidness our spiritual practices will liberate us, while to the extent that we do not realize it they will bind us.

Constant mindfulness of emptiness is the secret of success in the spiritual life. Only we must be careful not to discriminate emptiness from non-emptiness, since then it would not be emptiness but some kind of self-existence. True emptiness is empty even of the conception of emptiness. The void is itself void. Otherwise we fall into the heresy of nothingness.

Strangely enough, the remembrance of emptiness, far from decreasing one's power of spiritual activity, increases it enormously. It becomes easy, effortless, spontaneous, full of joy. Because the obstacle to activity, which is the self, has been removed.

The activity of the self is really not activity at all, and is always frustrated. The activity of emptiness is true activity, and is never frustrated.

The activity of emptiness is compassion.

Emptiness, activity, and compassion are not three things, but one thing looked at from three different points of view. Where one is present, the others will be present too.

He only can feel compassion for men who realizes that there are no men for whom to feel compassion. He only can serve who is free from the thought 'I serve'.

The remembrance of emptiness is fundamental.

The fool who rushes about trying to help the world without remembering that both he and it are void simply makes confusion worse confounded and tightens his own bonds. He who sits idle thinking that the conception of emptiness exempts him from activity and excuses the hardness of his heart that does not feel compassion falls into the heresy of nothingness and is doubly lost.

But he whose activities are boundless, whose compassion is infinite, and whose remembrance of emptiness is constant and unfailing, treads the Bodhisattva path and nears Nirvāṇa.

TIBETAN PILGRIMS

FROM THE DAZZLING WHITE WASTES of the Tibetan plateau, down through the steep and dangerous mountain passes, along the hot and dusty roads of what was once the Middle Kingdom, with sticks in their hands and sturdy backs bowed beneath the weight of heavy loads carried in wicker cradles suspended from their shoulders, with the sacred mantra *oṁ maṇi padme hūṁ* ever on their lips, in rough red homespun garments, knowing no other language than their own native Tibetan, by day and by night, year after year, impelled by their simple but profound faith, come these strange pilgrims from the far-off Land of Snows. *We* have come here with all the comforts and conveniences of a second-class railway carriage; but *they* have walked every single mile of the long road which stretches from their own country almost half-way across India here to Bodh Gaya. *We* admire the architecture of the Temple, speculate upon the probable date of its construction, and lament its present neglected and ruinous condition; but *their* simple faith pierces the diaphanous veil of such archaeological irrelevancies and is lost in the contemplation of the naked fact of the Lord's Enlightenment. Probably they are quite ignorant of the precise number of centuries which have passed by since he attained the sublime Consummation of His Noble Quest, and perhaps, were they questioned about it, they would scratch their tousled heads in surprise at the question and smilingly reply that they had never given thought to the matter; but from the evident earnestness with which they perform their devotions, from the unsophisticated sincerity of their demeanour, it seems as though that Great Event was as vivid and tangible to them as if the Lord had sat but yesterday upon the Diamond Throne and listened to the leaves of the Bodhi Tree whispering jubilantly above His head.

Some of the pilgrims are old, some young. Mostly they come in parties of four or five; but sometimes they arrive in pairs or singly. Some are dressed in garments of coarse red homespun cloth, with wide swinging skirts and full bosoms, and have ornaments of silver and turquoise around their necks and suspended from holes pierced in their ears; while others are clad in filthy black tatters that flutter and dance in the breeze, and wear strings of plain wooden beads. Some are shod with scarlet or yellow Chinese boots with upturned toes, while others – the poorer sort – go barefoot. Some are heavy laden with blankets, bags of rice, cooking utensils, and even little yellow-faced, rose-cheeked babies, suspended in wicker frames from their sturdy shoulders; and some carry miniature shrines of chased silver, through the tiny glass window of which is visible the gilded image of their tutelary Buddha or Bodhisattva within. A few of them carry long knives in ornamental silver scabbards slung at their side, and most of them have prayer-wheels, either tucked away idle in the capacious bosom of their dress, or twirling busily in their hand as they trudge along. But all of them, men, women, and children alike, are strongly and sturdily built, with round, smiling, rose-cheeked faces, cheerful salutations uttered in unfamiliar speech but with unmistakable friendliness, and hearts undaunted by the difficulties and dangers of their long and toilsome journey. They have walked perhaps a thousand miles, enduring with equal fortitude icy snow and burning sun; they have plodded on through wind and rain and dust, beholding now the dazzling white peaks of their native Himalayan ranges, now the swift-rushing streams and dense green foliage of the foothills, now the emerald rice-fields, barren burning plains, and dried-up river beds of India; and now at last they have reached their destination, and with broad smiles of greeting come stumbling through the gates of the Rest House. They have endured great hardships and many tribulations, experiencing not only the inclemency of nature but the cruelty and heartlessness of man; for some, taking advantage of the innocence and helplessness of these travellers in a strange land, have robbed and cheated them upon the way. Yet they do not complain; nor, now that they have at last arrived, do they look for compensating comforts, but spread their blankets on the cold stone floor of the veranda, or even bivouac out in the open air.

The clear blue winter sky and hard bright sunshine are perhaps even pleasant to them in comparison with the whirling snowstorms and icy cutting winds of their native land. Before an hour has passed they have kindled a fire and cooked thereon a frugal meal of rice-gruel flavoured with bits of chopped radish, onion, and chilli. Then they sit in democratic circle round their improvised kitchen and fill and refill their bowls with the steaming pottage that bubbles over the fire. They are easily satisfied, these simple pilgrim folk. They do not care for succulent dishes, nor rich clothes, nor yet for any of the luxuries which have become necessities to the pampered and perverted sons and daughters of modern city-bred civilization. Their food and clothing are simple but serviceable, even as their physical bodies are strong and sturdy, and their faith plain and unsophisticated. A casual glance might dismiss them with mingled contempt and disgust as simply ignorant and dirty. And it is indeed true that their clothes are black with grime, their hair as uncombed and thickly matted as the mane of a wild horse, and that they would perhaps have difficulty in remembering the date on which their skins last felt the contact of water. Neither are they educated in the sense in which we pride ourselves we are. Yet they carry in the bosom of their ragged, dirty garments a precious jewel which we, the doubt-torn, world-weary children of the twentieth century, would give much to possess – the precious jewel of faith.

True it is, indeed, that faith without knowledge breeds the rank and luxuriant growth of superstition, even as it is equally true that knowledge without faith conjures up the dismal spectres of doubt and scepticism. Yet it is perhaps less difficult for faith to give birth to knowledge than it is for knowledge to generate faith. Therefore we may well envy these simple people the possession of a faith which has enabled them to scale mountains and cross deserts, to suffer patiently and cheerfully for many months hardships which we could scarcely brook even for a single day. *Our* knowledge is a listless and anaemic thing: it does not inspire to great deeds of heroism and selfless love. But *their* faith is full of nerve and vigour: it kindles a warm and life-giving flame in their hearts, and with its beams illuminates their steps – even when they walk in a strange land. Therefore we may well wish that our complicated modern knowledge could be wedded to the simple faith of these Tibetan pilgrims – *prajñā* (wisdom) united to *karuṇā* (compassion) – that from their mystic union in our hearts might spring forth the glorious Bodhisattva of Buddha-ward aspiration.

Some of us might even wish that we could exchange our indigent and sterile knowledge for their rich and fruitful faith. But that may never be. We are the offspring of the twentieth century, they of the Ages of Faith – yet of a faith, surely, that is not blind, but founded on a deeper, truer knowledge belonging to the race, to the civilization, ultimately to the religion they profess itself, rather than to the individual believer. But we, for all our vaunted 'knowledge', grope and stumble in the dark; while they, for all their 'ignorance', walk along the road of life with humbly bowed but unwearied bodies, and slow but steady steps – walk as though the path beneath their feet and the destination at which they would one day arrive were both plainly visible before their eyes.

O, let us doff the glittering brocade of superficial modern intelligence, and don the coarse red homespun garment of simple faith! With the burden of long-suffering on our backs, and with the staff of endurance in our hands, let us join these humble pilgrims from the mysterious Land of Snows and trudge with them along the long and dusty road that leads to Bodh Gaya. With the Sacred Words on our lips, with the golden flame of faith and love burning in the transparent alabaster chalice of wisdom within our hearts, and with the Blessed One Himself for our guide, let us set forth as pilgrims upon the Middle Way that will lead us, one day, even to the Heart's Enlightenment.

NOTES

1 H.P. Blavatsky (trans.) *The Voice of the Silence*, Theosophical Pub. Co., London 1889.

2 A. Price (trans.) *Diamond Sūtra, The Jewel of Transcendental Wisdom*, p.26

3 *The Religions of the World*, Ramakrishna Mission Institute of Culture, 1938, vol.1, p.218

4 A.C. Bouquet, *Comparative Religion*, 1945, p.33

5 *Webster's New International Dictionary*, 2nd edition, London 1937.

6 Ibid.

7 *Aṅguttara Nikāya* i. 188 in F.L. Woodward, *Some Sayings of the Buddha*, p.189.

8 *Vinaya* ii. 10, in F.L. Woodward, *Some Sayings of the Buddha*, p.186.

9 A. Huxley, *Stories, Essays and Poems*, p.405.

10 For details of the derivation of emotions from love and hatred, and of these from desire, see Bhagavan Das, *Science of the Emotions*, 3rd edition, chapters III(B), IV, and V.

INDEX

The Windhorse symbolizes the energy of the enlightened mind carrying the Three Jewels – the Buddha, the Dharma, and the Sangha – to all sentient beings.

Buddhism is one of the fastest growing spiritual traditions in the Western world. Throughout its 2,500-year history, it has always succeeded in adapting its mode of expression to suit whatever culture it has encountered.

Windhorse Publications aims to continue this tradition as Buddhism comes to the West. Today's Westerners are heirs to the entire Buddhist tradition, free to draw instruction and inspiration from all the many schools and branches. Windhorse publishes works by authors who not only understand the Buddhist tradition but are also familiar with Western culture and the Western mind.

Windhorse Publications is an arm of the Friends of the Western Buddhist Order, which has more than sixty centres on four continents. Through these centres, members of the Western Buddhist Order offer regular programmes of events for the general public and for more experienced students. These include meditation classes, public talks, study on Buddhist themes and texts, and 'bodywork' classes such as t'ai chi, yoga, and massage. The FWBO also runs several retreat centres and the Karuna Trust, a fundraising charity that supports social welfare projects in the slums and villages of India.

Many FWBO centres have residential spiritual communities and ethical businesses associated with them. Arts activities are encouraged too, as is the development of strong bonds of friendship between people who share the same ideals. In this way the FWBO is developing a unique approach to Buddhism, not simply as a set of techniques, less still as an exotic cultural interest, but as a creatively directed way of life for people living in the modern world.

If you would like more information about the FWBO please write to

LONDON BUDDHIST CENTRE	ARYALOKA
51 ROMAN ROAD	HEARTWOOD CIRCLE
LONDON	NEWMARKET
E2 OHU	NEW HAMPSHIRE
UK	NH 03857
	USA

Also from Windhorse